THE LITTLE BOOK OF
MAGICAL CREATURES

THE LITTLE BOOK OF
MAGICAL CREATURES

The Little Book of Magical Creatures
Elizabeth Pepper & Barbara Stacy

Unless otherwise noted, all the pieces in
the "Storied Creatures" section are worldwide
folklore tales in new versions by Barbara Stacy.

The Witches' Almanac, Ltd.
Publishers Providence, Rhode Island

Address all inquiries and information to
THE WITCHES' ALMANAC, LTD.
P.O. Box 1292
Providence, RI 02840-9998

ISBN: 978-0-9773703-9-9

First Printing August 2009
10 9 8 7 6 5 4 3 2 1

Printed in Canada

A loving tribute to our creature kin,
from the tame to the wild to the fabulous.

The Witches' Almanac, Ltd.
Providence, Rhode Island

CONTENTS

Tame Creatures

Wild Creatures

Fabulous Creatures

Magic Storied Creatures

FOREWORD

Elizabeth Pepper told me that when she published the first *Witches' Almanac* in 1971, it was a labor of love. For me, writing this preface is a labor of love, too. *The Little Book of Magical Creatures* is a *Witches' Almanac* publication; I am honored beyond words to be associated with *The Witches' Almanac* in any small way.

I well recall the first time I encountered *The Witches' Almanac*. I don't remember exactly where I first saw it (it was in a book store, but I'm not sure which one) nor precisely when, other than it was in the 1970s and I was a teenager. I do recall exactly how *The Witches' Almanac* made me feel: *welcomed*. In its quiet, unpretentious way, *The Witches' Almanac* extended a welcome to all readers interested in any aspect of witchcraft and continues to do so to this day.

What I saw was a small, modest, paper-bound book *packed* with entertaining, informative mystic wisdom and enchanting illustrations. Its tone was (and remains) gracious, dignified, respectful, friendly, and often wickedly funny. Key words include "dignified" and "respectful": even now too many books address magic, witchcraft, witches, and magical creatures with mockery. Not Elizabeth Pepper and not *The Witches' Almanac*. If you have picked up this book because of love or fascination for living or mythic creatures, fear not: the subjects of this book are treated with unfailing respect as are readers whose intelligence is never doubted by the authors.

When it was suggested that I write *The Element Encyclopedia of Witchcraft*, I first demurred. Witchcraft is a hot-button topic full of arguments as to who is really a witch and what is really witchcraft. I wasn't eager to enter the fray. Then I considered witchcraft's many unsung heroes and heroines and the possibility that I could help shine a light upon them. Examples include Paschal Beverly Randolph, Franz Bardon, Moina Mathers, and especially Elizabeth Pepper and *The Witches' Almanac*.

The Little Book of Magical Creatures has sections devoted to tame creatures, wild creatures, fabulous creatures, and magic storied creatures, such as Brian Boru's horse and the Fenrir wolf. Among the most magical creatures of all, however, are those fabulous people who have bravely sought to keep magic traditions alive; Elizabeth Pepper and Barbara Stacy, authors of *The Little Book of Magical Creatures*, prominent among them.

The Witches' Almanac and its publications were Elizabeth Pepper's life work. A pioneer of magical publishing, she is responsible for a vast number of consistently affordable, entertaining, and charming books that are simultaneously steeped in ancient wisdom and as relevant to the modern day as any annual almanac must be. Most crucially, Pepper and the staff at *The Witches' Almanac* welcomed witches of all kinds, varieties, and persuasions, as well as any reader interested in witch lore, craft, and wisdom. So for newcomers to *The Witches' Almanac* and old friends alike: welcome to *The Little Book of Magical Creatures*.

JUDIKA ILLES, AUTHOR OF *PURE MAGIC, MAGIC WHEN YOU NEED IT, THE ENCYCLOPEDIA OF 5000 SPELLS, THE ELEMENT ENCYCLOPEDIA OF WITCHCRAFT,* AND *THE ENCYCLOPEDIA OF SPIRITS*

PREFACE

MYSTIC tradition grants pride of place to many members of the animal kingdom. Some share our life. Others live wild and free. Still others never lived at all, springing instead from the power of human imagination—many so vividly realized that we could easily identify them should we chance to meet.

Animals are magical beings, the subject of lore and legend from earliest time. Many achieved divinity and were worshipped as symbols of the highest virtues. Some were demonized by one culture and revered by another. Only certain animals qualified for otherworldly significance. Beauty, character, grace and symmetry were elements in the choice. And many possess a strange essence that clearly sets them apart from all the rest. We have collected their tales—our companions, the wild ones, and those wondrous fantasies that populate a world of delight and terror.

Animal Kingdom, Tobias Stimmer, 1576

Tame Creatures

If you really understand an animal so that he gets to trust you completely and, within his limits, understands you, there grows up between you affection of a purity and simplicity which seems to me peculiarly satisfactory. There is also a cosmic strangeness about animals which always fascinates me and gives to my affection for them a mysterious depth or background.

—LEONARD WOOLF

CATS

NCIENT Egyptians were the first to domesticate the feral cat, doubtless breeding smaller ones to rid the granaries of rodents and venomous snakes. Innate dignity, independent manner, elegant appearance and affectionate nature soon elevated the cat from servant to beloved household companion. By the time the Greek historian Herodotus visited Egypt in 445 BCE, the cat was established as the primary symbol of Bast, goddess of pleasure and music, especially noted for her magical power.

The worship of Bast reached its height during the reign of Osorkon II (874–853 BCE), when a magnificent temple to the cat goddess was built in the Nile Delta city of Bubastis, now in ruins and marked on contemporary maps as Tell Basta. Herodotus described the shrine and witnessed a festival honoring Bast attended by tens of thousands. He remarks on the

"obvious antiquity" of the ceremony and equates Bast with the
Greek goddess Artemis, for both
were lunar deities and represented feminine self-possession.
The Egyptian attitude toward
animals particularly impressed
Herodotus. Wild and tame creatures were all considered sacred,
and cats were deeply revered.
The spirit of Bast still appears
alive in modern Cairo, where

cats are ubiquitous. They roam the streets, hotel lobbies, museums, mosques, shops and government buildings, everywhere
treated with perfect kindness and infinite respect.

The ancient Egyptians so treasured their cats that exporting
them was strictly forbidden under Pharaonic rule. Despite the
ban, cats would eventually find their way throughout the
Middle East and into Western Europe. Persians and Greeks also
prized the cat as a protector of grain, and as such it accompanied
Phoenicians on sea voyages and Roman legions on their
conquests. Beyond its value as an enemy of rats is a certain mystical quality all cats possess. That essence is honored by some and
feared by others. Time hasn't changed the cat or our attitude
toward it. Someone once said that cats immediately recognize
whether people like or dislike them, and never care enough to do
anything about it. Perhaps the cat remembers its divine heritage.

Pagan associations would prove deadly to the cat as Christianity came to dominate the West. By medieval days felines

were regarded more often than not as demonic, companions of witches and servants of the devil. Themes in Celtic, Teutonic, and Scandinavian lore further linked cats with esoteric secrets and occult power. The love goddess Freya's chariot was drawn by two cats. Celts believed that a cat's eyes were windows through which an inner world could be explored. An 18th-century English witch described a ritual using a cat to cast a spell:

> *To be performed every evening, at the same place, at moonrise. Adapt your cat to sit close by you, facing the east. Stroke gently but firmly with love in your hands until its purrs and your breathing are heard as one sound. Now you and your cat possess the same will, your eyes will see alike, your thoughts will travel together. The time has come to work spells and cast enchantments, for power is doubled through the agency of your familiar creature.*

Folklore abounds in cat tales with shape-shifting a typical motif. Themes from fantasy become frighteningly real when we read an excerpt from testimony taken at the 1692 trial of Susanna Martin for witchcraft in Salem, Massachusetts. Witness Robert Downer swore that the accused had threatened his life and "that night as I lay in my bed, there came in at the window the likeness of a cat, which flew upon me, took fast hold of my throat, lay on me a considerable while, and almost killed me."

A prevalent belief held that witches could assume other forms. Reflecting it is a common tale with countless variations concerning a night-marauding cat discovered raiding a family larder and struck with a knife while escaping. The following day a highly regarded woman of the village is found to have a knife wound in her thigh. The stories of metamorphosis usually refer to women (cats and witches are most often perceived as female in folklore), yet one old tale told throughout Western Europe is about the King of the Cats:

A traveler passing the desolate ruins of an ancient church pauses to investigate an adjoining cemetery. As he crouches to study an old gravestone, his attention is caught by an odd sound — eerie yet somehow familiar. He peers around to see a curious procession of nine cats: one leads the way and the others, four on each side, carry a tiny black coffin. Resting on the coffin is an exquisite gold crown. The sound he hears is a kind of chant, for at every third step all the cats cry out together. The wayfarer hastens away to avoid being seen and reaches the home of an old friend at nightfall. In the cozy atmosphere of his friend's den, he relates the story of the strange sight he observed. As the visitor speaks, the cat curled up on the hearth becomes alert, stands up, stretches, and cries out: "Then I am King of the Cats!" and disappears up the chimney.

The true meaning of the cat's magical gifts may ever remain elusive. Despite thousands of years of close association, the cat is as mysterious to us today as it was when ancient Egyptians sensed its worth. A haunting feeling suggests that cats may know far more than they let on.

CATTLE

C HARGING across cave walls and ceilings, deep in the heart of the earth, are paintings of great herds of cattle. The brilliantly conceived images are the works of artists in Western Europe during Paleolithic times, around 15,000 BCE. People of this era hunted the animals and presumably the cave sanctuaries were scenes of sympathetic magic to promote a successful hunt. Or perhaps the painters simply created memorials to impress future generations. The many bulls and cows depicted belong to an extinct species of wild oxen, remote ancestors of modern cattle breeds. Evidence of the earliest domestic herds, over eight thousand years old, has been found in northern Greece and Turkey. From that time sustenance no longer depended on hunting and gathering, for humans developed stable food sources by keeping livestock and growing grain. Beef, milk, hides, and the strength to pull heavy plows required to till uncultivated soil were bovine benefactions.

Ancient cultures honored the bull for his vigor, fighting spirit, and sexual energy. As symbolic of fertility, the bull became associated with storms of wind and rain that activated parched earth. Bull cults arose throughout the Middle East and India. As a female aspect, the cow represented the loving mother, provider of nourishment and protection. The sacred nature of cattle was firmly established. In India today cows in particular are venerated.

Apis, the bull god of procreativity, was worshipped in Memphis, Egypt's ancient capital city. Old myths declare the god was immaculately conceived by a ray of moonlight, his horns an emblem of the Moon. Other sources say a thunderbolt descended upon a heavenly cow and brought forth Apis, a calf of solar power. Hathor, goddess of love, happiness, dance and music, was personified as a cow. An archaic deity, Hathor presided over childbirth. Both Apis and Hathor were portrayed crowned with the solar disk between two lunar horns representing the waxing and waning moon. Over many centuries Apis became associated with Osiris to form a dual god figure called Serapis by the Greeks. The worship of Serapis flourished throughout the Roman Empire, reaching as far north as York in England. Isis, female counterpart of Osiris, took on aspects of the cow goddess, often depicted wearing the horned crown.

On the island of Crete the bull defined masculine virility. Bronze Age murals of a bull-leaping sport suggest a link to

Spain's ritual of bullfighting. However, the restored frescos of Knossos have a playful air unrelated to the dark drama played out in the bullring. The bull often served as a sacrifice in early Mediterranean religious forms. Christianity's powerful rival Mithraism featured the solemn slaying of a bull in its mystic rites, and it seems more likely that bullfighting is rooted in that tradition. Crete was the home of the mythic Minotaur (half man and half bull), guardian of an underground labyrinth, his roar responsible for earthquakes.

Greek myths record that the great god Zeus disguised himself as a white bull to charm the maiden Europa. A romantic tale with a happy ending, for Zeus carried Europa over the sea to Crete, resumed his godlike form, and they found contentment together. His vengeful wife, the goddess Hera, apparently never got wind of the affair. Hera herself had bovine characteristics, for Homer often describes her as "cow-faced" and "cow-eyed." Another Greek tale has the beautiful Io, a maiden who caught the roving eye of Zeus, transformed into a white cow. Both myths are credited with naming the constellation of Taurus, a zodiac sign ruled by Venus and especially concerned with love and its many aspects.

Nordic cattle-rearing cultures found inspiration for their warriors in the bull's fierce nature. Horned helmets of the Vikings survive as proof of the affiliation. Celtic tribes in Ireland chose their king in an elaborate ceremony called the *tarbfeis*. A bull was slain, roasted and

TAME CREATURES

its meat and broth consumed as musicians played and priests chanted incantations. In the sleep following the feast, a dream would reveal the name of the future king to the presiding druid. Ancient Irish literature recounts the tale of an immense supernatural bull, the Donn of Cuailgne. Magic cows often appear in Celtic myths, most frequently white with red ears. Herds of cattle belonged to several deities, notably Flidais, the Celtic equivalent of the Greek goddess of the hunt, Artemis.

The horned beasts captured the imagination of people from the beginning of time. The raging bull in contrast to the docile cow, the destroyer and the nurturing protector became themes for art, drama, and poetry ranging from tragic expressions to the gentle musing of Robert Louis Stevenson in *A Child's Garden of Verses*:

> *The friendly cow all red and white,*
> *I love with all my heart:*
> *She gives me cream with all her might,*
> *To eat with apple tart.*

Europa and the Bull, Saragossa, 1488

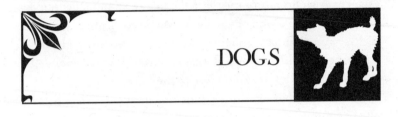

DOGS

A LINK is forged almost before conscious memory, born with the comforting nudge of a cold nose or recognition of sympathy in a pair of nonhuman eyes. And so begins a friendship that will never be forgotten. To experience the pleasure of a dog's company is one of childhood's finest gifts, for we learn to appreciate qualities rarely found elsewhere. Total acceptance, steadfast loyalty, joyful spirit, and unspoken understanding are canine characteristics.

Controversy exists over whether the wolf or the jackal or both are progenitors of the dog, but all agree that the dog is the earliest domesticated creature. Dog and human bonded during Neolithic times. The dog's primary function in prehistoric tribes was to protect the campsite, home and fields from intruders. Skills in hunting, retrieving, and herding developed until the animal became an indispensable partner in survival and later in sport, especially in royal sport. Paintings in Egyptian tombs depict elegant dogs—slender, sleek, swift—accompanying nobles in the hunt. The seventh-century BCE palace of the Assyrian warrior king Ashurbanipal at Nineveh displayed a splendid bas-relief of a great mastiff straining at his leash, eager for the chase.

Beloved and admired, the dog acquired magical associations throughout the ages and in an odd variety of cultures. In tribute, the ancients called the brightest star in the sky the Dog Star. Its other names, Sirius or Sothis, later would be identified with the goddess Isis. Hecate, Greek goddess of sorcery and Dark of the Moon, was said to travel with a retinue of black hounds. "Hark! her hounds are baying through the town," hailed Theocritus. Greek myths place Cerberus, the three-headed dog, on guard before the gate of the lower world. Roman household spirits, the Lares, were often joined by dogs. And with her loyal dog Garmr by her side, the Norse goddess Hel ruled the icy underworld of Nifelheim.

Teutonic legends tell of the Wild Hunt. On stormy nights the restless dead mount black steeds and with a pack of black hounds stream across the sky hunting human souls. Their leader is Woden or the Germanic sky goddess Holda. The lore would surface centuries later on Cornish moors, when high winds and rainy nights invoked the spectral Wisht hounds and their ghostly master. In full cry, the jet-black dogs sweep across Dartmoor and reputedly bring death to anyone unfortunate enough to meet them. The tale inspired Sir Arthur Conan Doyle's *The Hound of the Baskervilles*.

The dog's magical image increased when Agrippa, the great Renaissance occultist, traveled all over Europe with an enormous black mastiff as his constant companion. English court indictments recorded during the reigns of Elizabeth I and James I prove that "feeding and employing an evil spirit in the likeness of a dog" was a common basis for the charge of witchcraft. The dogs described were often black, but included a variety of sizes and colors—large or small, smooth or shaggy, spotted, white, yellow, gray or dun-colored. Anyone who shared hearth and home with a dog seems to have been fair game for the witch hunter. Fortunately, the terror of witch mania failed to diminish English devotion to canines.

The dog's role in folklore and literary fable continually shifts from dangerous to benevolent. There's a ghostly dog that appears out of nowhere to guide and protect a traveler passing through a dark wood or other treacherous terrain. When the journey ends and safety is assured, the dog vanishes into thin air. Another motif listed by scholarly index-makers is "Lean Dog Prefers Liberty to Abundant Food and Chain." A 20th-century example is English poet Irene Rutherford McLeod's virtual anthem of the "happy outsider."

LONE DOG

I'm a lean dog, a keen dog, a wild dog, and lone;
I'm a rough dog, a tough dog, hunting on my own;
I'm a bad dog, a mad dog, teasing silly sheep;
I love to sit and bay the moon, to keep fat souls from sleep.

I'll never be a lap dog, licking dirty feet,
A sleek dog, a meek dog, cringing for my meat,
Not for me the fireside, the well-filled plate,
But shut door, and sharp stone, and cuff and kick and hate.

Not for me the other dogs, running by my side.
Some have run a short while, but none of them would bide.
O mine is still the lone trail, the hard trail, the best,
Wide wind, and wild stars, and hunger of the quest!

GEESE

LARGE flocks of wild geese flying in V-shaped formation caught the attention of our ancients as the birds migrated south in the autumn only to return in springtime. Raucous cries from the geese announced their passage, true harbingers of the changing seasons. The Bronze Age drawing above is incised on a rock slab in a remote region of the Scottish Highlands and suggests spiritual significance. Norse folklore echoes the theme, for geese were traditionally sacrificed to the great god Odin at autumnal equinox.

A creation myth cherished by ancient Egyptians relates how Geb, the male earth deity, held the sky goddess Nut in loving embrace until rudely separated by a strong blast from Shu, god of winds. The concept of a masculine form for earth is unusual, as is the choice of a goose to symbolically represent Geb, one of Egypt's earliest gods. Egyptians were close observers of nature.

Did they note the process of imprinting, especially apparent in geese? Newly hatched goslings identify as nurturer the first moving object they see. The response to movement as the source of nourishment and protection reveals a profound truth about life on earth. Far away in time and place, Native Americans associated geese with the earth.

Classical myths honored the goose as sacred to Zeus/Jupiter and Aphrodite/Venus. And there's a famous tale about the geese that saved the garrison atop Capitoline Hill during Gaul's attack on Rome in 390 BCE. Around the precincts of the Temple of Jupiter, close to the crown of the hill, sacred geese stood guard. Fierce caretakers, geese are attentive to the slightest change in their environment. Scarcely had the Gallic warriors assembled for their assault before the geese trumpeted alarm, rising up and wildly flapping their wings to ward off the intruders. Aroused in time, the defenders won that battle. Geese still stand guard in some locales, sometimes more effectively than dogs or electronic warning systems.

Divinities are often depicted riding geese in many diverse cultures. Brahma rides the cosmic gander in the art of southern India. Aphrodite, Greek goddess of love, is shown riding a goose on a fifth-century BCE plate. The goddess Kosenko, borne by a goose in flight, is the subject of a lovely 18th-century Japanese print.

The favorite nursery character of Mother Goose has been linked to ancient goddess worship. Yet a bit of French royal gossip may be the true answer to her origin. Whispers had long flown around the court of Louis XIV that his queen, the naive Marie Theresa, had webbed feet. The rumor gave rise to an affectionate if patronizing nickname, Mother Goose. The first published collection of fairy tales, the 17th-century classic by Charles Perrault, carried frontispiece art captioned *Contes de ma mère l'oie*, tales of Mother Goose. How the nobles must have smiled behind their fans at the effrontery.

Mother Goose, Arthur Rackham, 1913

GOATS

WE HAVE these antic animals to thank for their nutritious milk, tangy cheese, and fine wools, including cashmere. Beyond these prosaic boons, goats can lay claim to rituals of the highest order. Among the ancients goats were revered sacrificial animals, chosen for rites that invoked magic to gain the attention of a god. The ceremony varied from culture to culture, but always there was the litany, always the knife, always the blood-spattered altar. Often the consecrated animal was roasted and consumed by the celebrants—death succeeded by life-affirming enjoyment. In Babylonia the priests wore sacred robes made from the skins of the sacrificial goats. As early as 1500 BCE the zodiacal image of Capricorn was established, with its head and body of a goat and a fish's tail. The Sea Goat appears engraved on

Chaldean gems, and a cuneiform inscription calls the goat "sacred and exalted."

For early Hebrews, the animal served in hallowed ritual at the Day of Atonement. Deemed Azazel, a wilderness demon, a female goat was chosen by lot and symbolically burdened with the sins of the people. Now ceremonially unclean, the hapless animal was driven into the wilderness to perish, the rite a yearly transfer of pollution to purify the community. Perhaps from this scapegoat practice arose a later tradition of the goat as a symbol of lust and evil.

In sharp contrast, northern Europeans revered the nimble goat for its playful nature. The love goddess of Germanic tribes rode a goat to May Eve revels. She held an apple to her lips, a hound and a hare ran beside her and a raven flew overhead. Thor, the red-headed Norse god of thunder, drove a chariot drawn by two fierce, unruly goats.

But the Greeks, the most wildly imaginative of storytellers, had their own notions about goats. Zeus, "most glorious, most great," owes his survival to Amalthea, a goat. Zeus was the son of the Titan Cronos, gigantic father of the gods, who feared the prophecy that one of his sons would dethrone him. To avert the calamity Cronos simply swallowed his progeny: Hestia, Demeter, Hera, Hades and Poseidon. When Rhea bore another son, she determined that he would escape the same fate. She held a rock in swaddling clothes to her breast, crooning a lullaby. Cronos bellowed at the sight, snatched the bundle and swallowed it, clothes and all. Rhea then sent the baby off to Crete in the care of Amalthea, who suckled Zeus and nourished him to glorious manhood. Her name was given to the

Aphrodite gambles with Pan, Greek, 4th century, BCE

legendary Horn of Plenty, the cornucopia from which flowed all desirable things.

As prophesied, the army of Zeus did mighty battle with the forces of Cronos as the skies thundered, the earth trembled, and tidal waves plunged. The young god Pan hailed the combat from the sidelines, shrieking with excitement. His shrill cries instilled such dread that they finally helped to rout the besieged Titans—the earliest case of inspiring "panic." Zeus prevailed and his siblings, freed from their peculiar prison, adjourned to Mount Olympus and chose him as their supreme ruler.

Pan also attended Dionysus/Bacchus, god of vegetation and of wine, in ecstatic revels celebrating the pure joy of being alive. The fertility deity Pan is depicted as a rough, lustful figure with the horns, legs and ears of a goat, and he often turns up with satyrs, also goat-men. Pan haunted pastures and enjoyed making people as well as cattle stampede in "panic." Twice yearly devotees of the nature cult whipped themselves into orgiastic frenzies of inspiration and of mystical ecstasy. The *orgia* invoked the cultists' unbridled animal nature and freedom from manmade restraints.

The revels reflected the dual nature of the god of wine, sometimes inspiring, sometimes unleashing dark forces. Beyond the wildness the woodland worship was simpler, providing adherents with relief from dusty city streets and hard labor. Living on herbs and berries, drinking from clear pools and sleeping on soft grass, the celebrants were renewed by the purity and beauty of the natural world. Four days later they would return refreshed to their families.

Oddly enough, we owe the art of drama to the Athenian music and dance festivals honoring Dionysus, whose symbol was the goat. The chorus and dancers wore goatskins and rites were traditionally orderly until a singer named Thespis entered into a dispute with the choral leader. The audience relished the lively verbal exchange. Thereafter a priest served as a speaker and entered into dialogue with the dancers, who evolved into the chorus in Athenian drama. Aeschylus had the brilliant idea to add a second speaker, and true theater was born. "Thespian" entered language as a term for actors; tragedy, the highest form of drama, means "goat song" in Greek.

But high comedy by way of goats prevailed during the Floralia, celebrated on April 28th in ancient Rome. The holiday was an erotic spring bash marked by lascivious performances in the Circus Maximus. To add to the festivity, goats as well as hares, both fertility symbols, were released amid the legs of the crowd, their frantic chase inspiring hysterical laughter. Spring fever is an old, old story.

HAWKS AND FALCONS

THE SOARING flight of a hawk is one of nature's most thrilling sights. Early Egyptians, observing the bird's dominion of the airy realm, referred to it as "God of the Sky." They named the hawk Horus and worshipped him before the dynasties began, believing that this bird's quality defined a vision of all that was worthy of respect and devotion. His right eye represented the Sun; his left, the Moon; the stars shone in his speckled plumage. Temple priests must have tamed and tended the wild birds, for they were depicted in ancient art perched on a block without tether, free to fly as they chose.

As the culture progressed, the sun god Ra evolved into the supreme deity. But the image of the hawk persisted in Ra's symbolic figure as a hawk-headed human wearing a sun disk on his head. The sky god Horus retained prestige by a mystical identification with royal power, and later artists added a pharaoh's crown to the hawk image.

Centuries passed and new legends bequeathed Horus to Isis and Osiris as their son, and over time the myth extended to portray the hawk god as the heroic avenger of his father. In Egypt, the hawk remained a spiritual presence in the sacred precincts of the temple, too revered a creature to be used for sport. The fifth-century BCE Greek historian Herodotus visited Egypt and noted: "For killing a hawk, whether deliberately or not, the punishment is inevitably death." The hawk was the primary symbol of honor, dignity, and supremacy for over the three thousand years of ancient Egyptian culture.

Other cultures revered the birds as superb hunting companions. Hunting with birds of prey originated in China around 2000 BCE, spreading westward to India, Arabia, and Persia over a long passage of time. The returning Crusaders introduced the hunting tradition to Europe and the British Isles, where it found great favor within the royal courts.

The words "falcon" and "hawk" are used interchangeably, but in the sport of falconry sharper distinction is drawn. The hawk is short

Royal Hawking Party, Paris, 1493

winged with bright yellow eyes; the falcon long winged with dark eyes. The bird favored by hunters is the female peregrine falcon. She is larger and more powerful than the male, as is the case with all the birds of this particular species.

But it isn't necessarily the hunter going forth with a hooded bird on his gauntleted wrist who experiences the richest pleasure of falconry. That must belong to those who tame and train the noble birds. One can imagine a spiritual kinship existing between the temple priests of ancient Egypt and their medieval counterparts preparing the birds for the field. Even today, the art is practiced in isolated regions where vast open countryside exists. Great patience, determination, and an intuitive gift are required to gain the trust and affection of wild creatures. This especially applies to hawks and falcons, by nature restless, moody birds. Long hours in darkened rooms, often late into the night, feeding and stroking the bird with a feather is the centuries-old method of taming. Feather-stroking is essential; oil from human skin can disturb the bird's plumage by removing a natural protective coating. A quiet meditative state, slow movement and soft words calm the bird during the process. And the reward far outweighs the effort, for the quality of an established rapport between human and bird is intensely satisfying—more than that, inspiring. A hawk inspired English poet John Skelton when he sought a creature to match the character of his beloved.

> *Merry Margaret,*
> *As midsummer flower,*
> *Gentle as falcon*
> *Or hawk of the tower.*

HORSES

HERE is no secret so close as that between a rider and his horse," said the English sportsman Robert S. Surtees. Mutual trust and understanding seem to exist beyond definable limits and reach a realm of cosmic strangeness. The presence of such a mysterious rapport ranks one of nature's most splendid creations in a class by itself.

Wild horses, ancestors of the domestic animal, still graze on Mongolian plains in diminishing number as the ancient species approaches extinction. Conquest and commerce brought the horse westward where it evoked awe and delight, its place in myth and legend assured.

The Hyksos, an errant horde of Asiatic horsemen, invaded and conquered Egypt in the 17th century BCE. The introduction of the horse and war chariot to the land of the pharaohs brought humiliating defeat. Nonetheless, Egyptians were captivated by the quality and potential of the animal. Two hundred years passed before the Hyksos were expelled, but during that time Egyptians became proficient in breeding and tending horses. Empire builder Thutmose III, who ruled from 1479 to 1425 BCE, rejoiced over his son's passion for the animal: "Now when he was a lad, he loved his horses, he delighted in them, he was persevering at exercising them and knowing their ways, skilled in training them." The Pharaoh ordered his retinue: "Let there be given to him the very best horses of the stable of his majesty which is in Memphis. Tell him to take care of them." Thutmose revealed a basic equestrian truth, for it is not enough to ride well. Devotion to care is essential in order to win the confidence of high-strung and sensitive creatures. Too late an arrival to garner religious significance, the horse was beloved and treasured for its uncanny awareness of the unseen.

The ancient Greeks were equally charmed by the horse. It has been said that the first sight of a horse and rider inspired the concept of the mythological centaur—half man and half horse. Myths credit Poseidon, god of the sea, with creation of

the first horse during a contest with Athena. Zeus decreed that whichever deity created the most useful object to mankind should have the honor of naming a beautiful new city. Athena dreamed up the olive tree, won the contest, and named the site Athens. But it must be conceded that Poseidon's creation is more universally valuable. Many tales are told of the winged horse Pegasus, sired by Poseidon and born of Medusa, whose sacred duty was to carry thunder and lightning to Zeus on Mount Olympus.

The *ashvamedha* or horse sacrifice, a reflection of earlier Scythian horse offerings to the Sun, was a distinctive Indian ceremony from 1000 to 50 BCE. In Hindu lore the horse often represented Surya, the Sun god. Epona (Divine Horse) was worshipped in Gaul as goddess and protector of horses by Celtic tribes.

White horses were sacred symbols in the British Isles. A prehistoric hill figure known as the Uffington White Horse, some 360 feet in length, gallops across the Berkshire Downs. Cut into turf to expose the chalk beneath, the White Horse was for centuries scoured every seven years during an ancient festival of unknown origin. Some scholars connect the monument with Gaul's Epona. Others speculate that the White Horse is a tribute to the Welsh goddess Rhiannon. Odin, the dominant god of Scandinavian legend, rode the eight-legged steed Sleipnir, faster than the wind, on his visits to the land of the dead. Another Norse myth tells of Alsvidur, the all-swift horse, which drew the chariot of the Moon goddess.

Fleetness is but one of the qualities admired in the horse. Ancient people believed that the fastest mares were with foal from the winds. Folklore holds that horses possess clairvoyance, often refusing to proceed or shying mysteriously when no visible obstacles are in view. They are believed especially susceptible to the Evil Eye and in Italy are often adorned with brass amulets to avert the *jettatora*.

The horse owns a year in the Oriental zodiac. Its natives are deemed spirited, often possessing peculiar psychic power. Mystical themes regarding the horse are prevalent throughout the world. The wonderfully strange communication achieved between human and equine continues to be an elusive factor.

27

PEACOCKS

BEAUTY is the keyword to define the magical peacock. A spectacular train of iridescent feathers—purple, blue-green, copper, gold and bronze—is the pride of the adult male bird. The glory of his train fanned out in courting display excites the peahen, assuring the continuation of the species. And it is the shimmering beauty of peacock plumage that has always attracted human admiration.

Native to India, the peacock attained divinity in Hinduism, for its qualities symbolized Indra, god of thunder, rain, and war. Reasons for the association are evident. The peacock's courtship ritual includes an ear-splitting scream. Breeding season occurs just before India's summer monsoons, and the raucous cries herald rain. The peacoke is a fierce fighter and predator of snakes. Its powerful claws and iron beak equip the bird to successfully dispatch a cobra or other poisonous reptiles.

Chosen as the Indian national bird in 1963, peacocks continue to enjoy the favored status conferred since Asoka, third-century BCE emperor, decreed a limit on their slaughter. Peacock feathers are emblems of strength and good fortune throughout the East. In the West, a contrary theme developed.

The semi-tame bird has a sedentary nature and is content in captivity as long as food, water, and a comfortable environment are provided. Nobility of ancient kingdoms imported pairs to breed, and peacocks graced the gardens of Babylon, Egypt, Persia, and Greece. Alexander the Great so admired the bird that he imposed heavy fines on individuals hunting them as game. The Greeks associated peacocks with the goddess Hera, queen of heaven.

Hera's role in early Greek myth is singularly unpleasant. She was depicted as a beautiful woman, but proud, insanely jealous, vindictive, cold and cruel beyond measure. Her primary concern was to punish women with whom her husband Zeus dallied. One myth relates that Zeus transformed his lover Io into a white heifer to allay Hera's suspicion. But she, accustomed to his trickery, demanded the cow as a gift. The guilty Zeus agreed. When Hera set Argus of One Hundred Eyes to guard the creature, Zeus sent his clever son Hermes to retrieve Io. Hermes lulled all One Hundred Eyes to sleep with music, slew Argus and set the heifer free. When she discovered the crime, Hera gathered up the eyes of Argus and in a towering rage flung them over the long train of her peacock—ever to serve as a reminder of the treachery.

Another characteristic of Hera was vanity. A peacock's first priority upon waking is to fastidiously preen its feathers. A notable passage in Homer's *Iliad* describes Hera grooming herself to seduce Zeus, whose love for her had grown cold. Her success changed the course of the Trojan War.

The reputation of the peacock suffered as a result of its identification with Hera. The "eyes" of its plumage came to symbolize the Evil Eye. Many Western occult traditions regard peacocks as omens of ill fortune and their feathers as tokens of bad luck.

But perhaps beauty alone is reason enough to cherish the bird. In a sixth-century BCE fable of Aesop, the peacock complains to Hera that while the nightingale pleases every ear with its song, a peacock's cry is met with laughter. The goddess consoles him, "But you far excel in beauty and size. The splendor of the emerald shines in your neck, and you unfold a tail gorgeous with painted plumage." Her answer fails to satisfy the peacock and he asks, "But for what purpose have I this dumb beauty so long as I am surpassed in song?" Hera explains that the lot of each bird is assigned by the will of the Fates: "To thee, beauty; to the eagle, strength; to the nightingale, song; to the raven, favorable, and to the crow, unfavorable, auguries. Be content with your lot; one cannot be first in everything."

Peacock display, Zurich, 1560

ROOSTERS

PHRODITE, goddess of love, and Ares, god of war, engaged in an illicit love affair. To be sure that their meetings were kept secret, a youth named Alectryon promised to keep watch and give warning should anyone approach. Unfortunately, Alectryon fell asleep. The Sun rose, spied the lovers, and reported the adultery to Hephaestus, Aphrodite's husband. Since he was the god of metal-working, Hephaestus took revenge for the affront by forging a wondrously fine net and casting it over the guilty pair. Aphrodite and Ares, unable to escape, were exposed to the delight and ridicule of their fellow Olympians. When finally released, a furious Ares transformed Alectryon into a rooster and banished him to the barnyard, decreeing that ever after he must crow at sunrise. From this myth, recounted by Homer in the *Odyssey*, came the Greek word *alektryon*, cock, and the bird's role as herald of dawn.

The cock is ruler of a large harem of hens, noted for his feisty spirit, and his destiny is intertwined with love and war. Anyone who has gathered eggs from a hencoop can testify to a rooster's aggressive nature. Ancient warriors of the Middle East wore helmets adorned with a crest that has been likened to a cockscomb, and similar gear was displayed down to Roman times. Such a headpiece might imbue a soldier with the bird's courage and pugnacity. Cockfighting, a bloody battle to the death, was an early form of entertainment and still has its adherents.

When the sun rose and dispelled darkness, human spirits were lifted. Dawn, some say, is the enemy of evil. When it became the cock's crow that pronounced the end of night, the bird himself was regarded as a solar symbol. His image appeared on coins, amulets, and weathervanes. Helios and Apollo, Greek gods of the Sun, and the goddess Persephone, personification of rebirth and springtime, received the cock as an emblem. Depictions of the bird are absent from the tombs and temples of ancient Egypt because the fowl was not introduced in that land until 1400 BCE. The Romans dedicated the rooster to Mercury in his role as god of commerce. At the turn of the Common Era, the Gnostic sects of Alexandria portrayed their Sun god Abraxas with a cock's head.

The rooster is an Oriental bird. Its common ancestor is the Red or Indian Junglefowl, *Gallus ferrugineus*, native to southern Asia. We might expect the bird to hold sacred significance in the East, where he rules a year of the Chinese lunar calendar. As one of the twelve creatures to whom Buddha granted the power to bestow its own characteristics upon those born in its time span, the cock year gives its natives flamboyance, self-assurance, an aggressive nature, and a devotion to minutia. A Ming Dynasty sculpture of *feng-huang*, a magical bird of Chinese legend, bears a strong resemblance to the rooster. As the most exalted of the four spiritual creatures—tortoise, unicorn, dragon—*feng-huang* only appeared in times of peace and prosperity.

SHEEP

O N A STEEP cliff wall in Algeria where the Sahara Desert meets the Atlas Mountains is a remarkable engraving made over seven thousand years ago. An enormous ram towers over a man whose arms are raised as if in awe. The ram wears a decorative neck band and is crowned with a large disk from which rays emanate. This area was once fertile land where herds of wild sheep grazed and the ram commanded interest and respect.

The image portends the sanctity the ram would eventually hold farther east in the Nile Valley. In ancient Egypt's pre-dynastic times Khnemu, a god associated with creation, was portrayed as a ram or a ram-headed man crowned with the solar disk. The great god Amon, whose worship combined with the power of the Sun god, Ra, claimed the ram as his symbolic creature. The massive complex of ruins at Karnak includes a magnificent avenue of ram-headed sphinxes leading to the Great Temple of Amon-Ra. God of gods, Amon-Ra signified a mysterious hidden force that created and sustained the universe. Greek and Roman visitors would equate Amon-Ra with their chief god Zeus/Jupiter.

The Roman astrologer and poet Manilius credits the Egyptian priesthood with the development and refinement of astrology. And it may be due to the prestige of Amon-Ra that Aries the Ram is the first sign of the zodiac. "Resplendent in his golden fleece the Ram leads the way," wrote Manilius around the turn of the Common Era. The "golden fleece" refers to the ram of Greek myth that saves two children from death and is then sacrificed to the gods, his fleece later becoming the prize sought by Jason and the Argonaut expedition. The astrological personality assigned to the Ram in the West is bold and audacious. The Sheep of Oriental astrology displays far different characteristics. Natives of a Sheep Year are gentle souls, never forceful or dynamic.

Sheep were among the world's earliest domesticated animals, and their contrary gender images—strong male and meek female—surfaced in various cultures down the ages. The Hebrews honored the male's power in wartime and in religious ritual. The shofar, a ram's horn, was once used for its blare to issue battle signals, and is still to be heard in synagogues over the High Holidays. Christianity favored the more serene sheep, and the themes of the shepherd and his flock, the purity and innocence of the lamb, appear often in church doctrine. In the Roman Catholic Church, bishops carry the crosier, or shepherd's crook, as an emblem of their pastoral duty toward their human flocks.

SWINE

THE MAGICAL history of the pig is paradoxical, sometimes receiving its due as an excellent creature, sometimes reviled. Through the ages the wild boar was universally renowned for courage and intelligence. Domestication occurred first in China, where the pig was accorded respect. Representing a year in the Oriental astrological cycle, a boar native would be indolent, honest, generous, and a seeker of harmony. Buddhist lore pronounces the pig lazy and vulnerable to attack, but pig talismans are often used in the Orient and India to ward off angry demons. Another porcine image appears in the Hindu creation myth relating how Vishnu, incarnated as the boar Varaha, raises the earth goddess from the primeval sea.

The pig's fate swung from divine to abominable when Semitic tribes of the Levant herded swine. Hebrews were forbidden to kill or eat pigs, a dictum interpreted by some scholars as evidence that the animals were originally considered sacred. A biblical admonition to refrain from casting pearls before swine clearly indicates a marked aversion to the animal. Arabs shared the same attitude, for the Koran prohibits eating pork. Some historians suggest that since pork becomes rancid without refrigeration in hot climates, the religious dietary laws merely reflect an awareness of the danger. But even in Egypt where most animals were revered, a piglike creature portrayed the evil god Set—he who cut the grain Osiris planted. Pork was traditionally eaten only once a year at the Midwinter Feast, and those who tended swine were considered unfit to enter the temples of the gods. The theme that pigs are unclean prevailed throughout the Middle East despite the fact that the animals are by nature fastidious.

The pig's fortune improved in Greece, for it was deemed sacred to Demeter, goddess of vegetation. And although the wild boar was notorious for ravaging crops, it was credited as well with teaching farmers to churn up the earth. Greek myths associate the pig with purity and protection from evil spirits. Apollo raised a pig above the head of Orestes to absolve him of guilt for the death of his mother. Initiates to the Eleusinian Mysteries, the highest spiritual rite of ancient Greece, used the pig in liturgy. They took charge of a young pig and ceremonially washed both pig and themselves in the sea on the journey from Athens to Eleusis, where they would comprehend Demeter's mystic truths. According to Homer, the fair-haired sorceress Circe was so offended by the ill manners of Odysseus' ravenous crew that she transformed them into swine. The colorful fiction lives on to give pigs an undeserved reputation for greed.

Pigs fared better in northern Europe. Scandinavian legends honored the boar as a formidable enemy. Warriors carried shields emblazoned with a boar's head as a protective emblem. Nordic tribes, hoping to be imbued with the animal's valor, feasted on roast pork. A magnificent golden boar named Gollinborsti (Goldenbristles) belonged to the Norse deities Freyr and Freya. The Celts especially sensed the animal's otherworldly qualities. Supernatural boars and magical pigs abound in their myths. The Welsh tale of Twrch Trwyth, a king transformed into a great boar, is a notable example. King Arthur and his men hunted the beast for the mysterious treasure he held between his ears.

Nuggets of ancient wisdom survive in folklore and rural customs. Pigs are believed to understand the voice of the wind and can predict the weather. Porcine intelligence and response to music confounds some people with fear of devil possession. A persistent motif contends that the words "pork" and "bacon" must not be mentioned within the hearing of swine. Wise farmers pay heed.

Apollo purifies Orestes, Greek, 5th century BCE

Wild

Creatures

We share the planet with thinking animals. Each
species, with its uniquely sculpted mind, endowed by
nature and shaped by evolution, is capable of meeting
the most fundamental challenges that the physical and
psychological world presents. Although the human
mind leaves a characteristically different imprint on
the planet, we are certainly not alone in this process.

— MARC. D. HAUSER

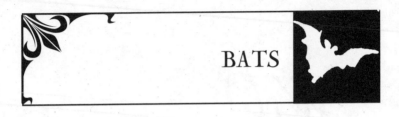

BATS

I N THE PERFECT system that is the natural world, bats are perhaps the most vilified. They are virtuous little creatures that provide us with a variety of enormous benefits. Without bats on the job, we would be shrouded in insects. Worldwide, bats are the most voracious destroyers of flying pests, able to gobble as many as six hundred mosquitoes in an hour. In Texas the furry flyers repay hospitality by wiping out about twenty thousand tons of insects a year. Farmers in the Southwest and in tropical climates, where cacti and other plants flower at night, welcome bats for the sexual courier service of moving pollen from blossom to blossom.

But misconceptions are rife. Neither birds nor rodents, bats are members of the order *Chiroptera*, "hand wing," the only mammals to have evolved true flight. Their sheer numbers are stunning; nearly one thousand species account for about one quarter of all mammals.

At night bats emerge from their sunless sleeping quarters, caves or dark spaces in buildings, and flap out to feed. They scare people by flying with mouths agape and little teeth glistening, a sight that in no way signifies aggression. The creatures are squeaking to "see" by echolocation. Similar to sonar, the method works so beautifully that bats can evade a thread strung in the pitch dark, which puts to rest another eerie fallacy—that bats fumble their way into women's hair. Amanda Lollar, author of *The Bat in My Pocket,* is enchanted by bats. Lollar met her first as she gingerly tended the injured creature and became charmed with the bat's quirky character. The author discovered that her "troll doll" had an irresistibly mischievous, loving personality and surpassed dogs and cats in intelligence. "She had a reaction to everything," Lollar wrote, "excitement, boredom, happiness, hunger or affection.

All of them could be read on her face, and her chitterings took on different notes to match these emotions."

Historical records show a dearth of bat pets, but conflicting beliefs do turn up in ancient cultures. The Chinese believed that bats were lucky, and further maintained that they flew head downwards to accommodate the weight of their brains. Some Africans considered bats sacred, embodying the souls of the dead. Native Americans used them in initiation rituals, symbolizing rebirth as creatures emerging from the dark cave of Mother Earth's womb.

But bats have long had mysterious and terrifying associations. To the Irish the bat is a death symbol, and a flying phantom to the aborigines of British Columbia. In most of the world the entry of a bat into a house portends the death of an occupant. In medieval times people believed that the Devil assumed the shape of a bat, entered the human body, and only exorcism could rid the victim of the fluttering monstrosity.

Which brings us to vampire bats. An obscure species of tiny toothless South American bats does seek the blood of cattle and small mammals, but has no taste for the human neck. The foundation of today's vampire craze began with the publication of Bram Stoker's *Dracula*, which itself never stressed the bat connection. The mischief has been cinematic. In 1922 the eerie legend turned up in the German Expressionist film *Nosferatu, A Symphony of Horror*, followed nine years later by the Bela Lugosi *Dracula*, a runaway hit, with the undead's black cape morphing into bat wings. Since then there have been many films with bats featured as purveyors of terror — and reinforcing the dark beliefs.

BUTTERFLIES

THE CHILEAN poet Neruda calls them "flying violets," a child friend calls them "flutterbys." Whatever the terminology, our hearts lift at the sight of a butterfly, the essence of beauty and freedom. The Greek word "psyche" means both "soul" and "butterfly," and since ancient times the elegant airborne creature has symbolized rebirth. Its own life cycle is a dazzling metamorphosis. The butterfly begins as a caterpillar and transforms into a pupa enclosed in a cocoon. Inside the form-fitting home it modifies, struggles out, shakily unfolds itself and flies off with the simultaneous wings rippling. Nourishment is simplicity itself, requiring only nectar. Milkweed, verbena and red clover delight the butterfly, which alights on the flower and uncoils its long tongue to sip the refreshment. The gorgeous creature will live only a month, a short but blithe life.

To the imaginative Greeks the soul took two butterfly forms. In its earliest image the soul was depicted as a tiny person with butterfly wings like a fairy; later a butterfly itself signified the soul. An uncanny similarity of the butterfly/spirit link exists in almost as many places as clouds of butterflies bless with their presence. Some Germans believe that the dead are reborn as children who fly as butterflies. In Assam, Nagas assert that death brings a number of transformations in the underworld, ending with rebirth as a butterfly. The dying man chooses his form of rebirth in the Solomon Islands, and butterflies are the favored choice. And in sites as scattered as Cornwall, Siberia and Mexico, white butterflies inspired the most awe as repositories of dead souls. But Finns and others believe that the butterfly-soul can vacate the body while a person sleeps, accounting for dreams. And the Serbs have unique associations with sleep, butterflies and witchcraft. If they can find a sleeping witch and turn the body around without waking her, the soul will be unable to find the mouth for reentering its abode and the witch will die.

Butterflies also flutter their way into some creation myths. A Sumatran tribe claims descent from three brothers hatched from butterfly eggs, although they married heavenly wives sent down fully grown. Legends of the Pima tribe of Arizona declare that Chiowotmahki, the Creator, transformed itself into a butterfly and flew over the world until it found the optimum place for mankind.

Similarity also exists in a few places where people believe butterflies are taboo. Their cousins the moths are widely regarded as malicious witch spirits, and sometimes the disfavor extends to butterflies. In medieval Westphalia, St. Peter's Day featured a tradition of butterfly banishment. Children ran around the villages knocking on houses with hammers and reciting incantations to drive the creatures outside. Perhaps the reason for this obviously mock ritual is the ancient belief that butterflies steal the butter.

Capture is viewed as bringing luck in some places, usually with a brief ritual. In the German town of Oldenburg, the first butterfly of the season should be caught and flown through your coat sleeve. If you spot the first white of the season in Essex, England, tradition directs you to bite off its head but allow it to fly away. It's our guess that many a blind eye must be turned toward the first white butterfly. Folks in Suffolk tell us that you must "tenderly entreat" the resplendent captive. Nice idea. Next time you find one of the beauties, watch it for a moment, wish it a blissful nectar-filled life, and voice your own hope for the same.

CROWS
AND RAVENS

YOU PROBABLY never have pondered until you were weak and weary about the nature of ravens and crows, but these seemingly ordinary creatures have an amazing mythology. Sometimes the raven, *Corvus corax*, is singled out, sometimes the crow, *Corvus brachyrhynchos*. The stories vary from their guises as creators of the world to sinister forces to oracles, especially in deciding the fate of soldiers in combat. The birds also feature in a flock of accounts as raucous practical jokers, perhaps derived from their actual playful natures. Crows and ravens enjoy chasing each other in sky acrobatics and have been known to buzz dogs, cats and sometimes people, apparently whooping it up just for fun.

From Siberia to North America, Crow and his big brother Raven star in an ancient cycle of creation myths. The Haida of the Queen Charlotte Islands, for instance, believed that a huge Raven created mankind. At first Raven flew alone, but solo flight became lonely and he wanted companions. He spotted a clam shell on the shore and spit on it. By and by he heard voices from the shell, pried it open with his beak, and freed the first human beings. In many genesis stories Raven imparted his own greedy, irreverent spirit to all he touched. Legend has it that as a final joke he added genitals to the creatures he made, "Raven's greatest game."

In some tales the sooty bird originates as a beautiful white bird, an attendant on gods and heroes. Such a crow, white as milk, served as Apollo's oracular bird. When the god fell in love with the mortal Coronis, he suspected that she was unfaithful and commanded the crow to spy her out. When the bird flew back with a report of her dalliance with Ischys, Apollo was enraged at the messenger as well as the lovers. Since the bird had failed to blind Ischys with its sharp beak, as crows were believed to do when irked with humans, Apollo turned the crow black—from ancient times the color of death and disaster.

A tale from Native Americans also accounts for transformation to the dusky color. The Raven-Who-Sets-Things-Right was a pure white bird who reclaimed the earth from wasteland to paradise for the first humans. The Old One, a rich miser who lived at the end of the earth, hoarded the fresh water, food and fire. Raven stole the elements and from them created mountains, forests, rivers and streams, stocking them with animals and fish. And to enhance the human condition further and deliver man from bleak darkness, he stole the Old One's bag of moon and stars and flung them into the sky. But during one of the burglaries, he was caught in the smoke hole of the tent and hung helpless until his gleaming white feathers were coated with an everlasting sootiness.

An elaborate mythology about the birds wove its way into Celtic and Norse lore, often as superb battlefield magic. Early Danes fought under a pure white banner until the heat of battle, when a raven would appear on the flag; its wings drooped if the Danes were doomed, spread wide to presage victory. Mighty Odin himself kept company with two ravens, Thought and Memory, one perched at each shoulder. At first light they flew into the world, swiftly circling the globe in opposite directions and checking out the follies of mankind. When they returned to Valhalla, the ravens croaked the news of the day into the god's ears. The Morrigan, "Great Queen," is the Celtic goddess of battle and fertility. In old, old stories she turns up either as a single entity or as a trio with Badb and Macha, all of whom hover over the combat in the guise of crows cawing incantations. Perhaps one was "nevermore," the most unlucky word Poe could imagine. But in the epic *Beowulf*, the black bird heralds sunrise.

> *The black-coated raven,*
> *Blithesome of spirit,*
> *Hailed the coming of Heaven's bliss.*
> *Then over the shadows uprose the sun.*

In tales menacing or benevolent, crows and ravens are never depicted as bird brained; much mythology reflects their very real intelligence. "If men had wings and bore black feathers, few of them would be clever enough to be crows," declared the

19th-century theologian Henry Ward Beecher. The ultimate cleverness of crows is reflected in Aesop's famous fable: "A thirsty crow found a pitcher with some water in it, but so little was there that, try as she might, she could not reach it with her beak, and it seemed as though she would die of thirst within sight of the remedy. At last she hit upon a clever plan. She began dropping pebbles into the pitcher and with each pebble the water rose a little higher until at last it reached the brim, and the bird was enabled to quench her thirst." That was one smart crow, but one could expect nothing less from a Corvid.

Aesop's Fables, Arthur Rackham, 1912

DEER

LEGANT, swift, shy and elusive describe one of the world's most beautiful animals. Thirty-four species of deer have adapted to environments from arctic to tropic in North and South America, Europe, northwest Africa and Asia. Wherever deer exist, people have told mystical tales about them.

The earliest hint of their otherworldly nature is a striking rock painting known as the Sorcerer, c. 12,000 BCE. Deep in the cavern of Les Trois Frères in southern France a human figure wearing antlers dominates a wall covered with engravings of myriad animals. The stag and his antlers, both widely regarded as supernatural, have ever been associated with shamans and many forms of pagan worship.

The theme of transformation constantly occurs in deer legend and folklore. The Greek goddess of the hunt, Artemis, favored deer above all creatures and displayed a cruel streak

Artemis, Ernst Lehner, 1912

when she took revenge on a hapless hunter. Actaeon's only sin was to accidentally glimpse the goddess and her nymphs bathing in a mountain pool. Artemis was so offended at being observed naked by a mere mortal that she sprayed Actaeon with water which turned him into a stag doomed to be killed by his own hounds.

An old English legend with deer and metamorphosis as the primary motif concerns Lady Sybil of Bernshaw Tower in Lancashire. She was beautiful, wealthy, "intellectual beyond most of her sex," and irresistibly drawn to the practice of witchcraft, for which she showed remarkable talent. Lady Sybil loved nature with all her heart and enjoyed nothing so much as to ramble through the deep ravines of Cliviger Gorge in the form of a milk-white doe. One May Eve in this guise she was captured by Lord

William of Townley Castle with the magical help of another Lancashire witch, the famous Mother Helston.

It all began in early spring a very long time ago. Lord William had nearly despaired of ever winning the lovely heiress of Bernshaw Tower as his bride. She was indifferent to his courting and repeatedly spurned his advances.

Albrect Dürer, 1500

But Mother Helston prepared a powerful spell woven into a long silken chord and loaned Lord William her own familiar, a fierce black hound. With these the nobleman won his heart's desire, for at cock's crow the captive doe became Lady Sybil, now docile and subject to his will. But Lord William made a fatal mistake when he offended Mother Helston by failing to properly thank her for her efforts on his behalf.

Within one passage of the Moon the spell was lifted and Lady Sybil sought her freedom. Lord William was forced to hold her prisoner under the constant guard of his manservant Robin. One night while Robin dozed a splendid white cat tried to slip by him. Robin woke with a roar and with his dagger struck off the cat's paw. When he stooped to pick it up, in its place lay the severed hand of Lady Sybil, identified by an elaborate diamond ring on her forefinger. The hand was returned to its owner and magically restored to Lady Sybil's arm, although a faint red line remained. Lord William tried his best to make amends, but it was too late. The lady's health declined after this episode and she soon died.

According to her wishes, Lady Sybil was buried in Cliviger Gorge close by Eagle Crag, where as the white doe she had been run to ground by Mother Helston's hound. And when darkness falls on May Eve, so the legend tells, doe and hound and ardent hunter return to haunt the night.

DOLPHINS

PEOPLE tend to take dolphins into their hearts and the affection seems requited, for of all wild creatures these are especially enticed by our voices and music. Sailors rejoice in the sight of dolphins crashing through the waves and submerging like sleek little submarines, the swiftest of sea travelers. They plunge along at speeds of up to eighteen miles an hour, bottle noses cleaving the water, ever seeming to smile. Their intelligence is notable, and they clamor in complex whistles, clicks and clacks that madden scientists aspiring to break the language barrier.

The felicitous creatures have been committing random acts of kindness to humankind since antiquity. Old tales abound of dolphins rescuing swimmers, allowing children to ride their backs, herding schools of fish toward nets. Dolphins could even be summoned, the Roman historian Pliny tells us—when certain fishermen would shout *simo*, "snub nosed," dolphins often emerged as fishing companions and helpers.

Greek and Roman mythology is awash in dolphin tales. In one story Dionysus, the god of wine, hires a ship to cross the sea. Unaware of his identity, the crew plot to capture him and sell him into slavery. When Dionysus discovers the scheme, he manifests by flooding the ship with wine, sounding shrieking music like gale winds, turning the oars into snakes and the mast into a tangle of grapevines. The terrified sailors leap into the sea, where Poseidon transforms them into dolphins.

The creatures are associated with love and beauty — Eros and Aphrodite are often depicted riding dolphins. But the most potent legend associates dolphins with divine wisdom in their bond with Apollo, god of sunlight, music and the sacred mysteries of Delphi. On that site, originally called Pytho, a monstrous beast guarded a prophetess who inhaled trance-inducing vapors from a spring. When the Python arose from his lair beside the sanctuary, he lumbered out to terrorize the countryside, killing villagers and destroying crops. Apollo "killed the fearsome dragon Python, piercing it with his darts," as Homer tells us. But the monster was the son of the goddess Gaia, and as punishment for the kill Apollo was compelled to serve seven years as a cowherd in a distant land. When he wished to return, the deity assumed the guise of a dolphin, leaped aboard a Cretan ship and received passage. The site was renamed Delphi in honor of the dolphin, *delphis*, and Apollo took possession of the spring. Now often termed Apollo Delphinius, he bestowed divine powers on its priestess, who chewed laurel leaves as she muttered ambiguous oracles.

Delphi, the prime Apollonian cult site, became the most powerful oracular center of the ancient world.

The dolphin also has a Poseidon connection. The lusty deity with the roving eye wished to possess the nereid Amphitrite. But she distrusted the sea god, known to play unattractive practical jokes with squid, jellyfish and octopus. Amphitrite fled to the mountains, but her persistent lover sent numerous messengers pleading his amorous cause. Finally, curiously enough, it was a beguiling dolphin that won her heart for Poseidon and Amphitrite returned to the underwater realm as queen of the sea. The grateful god thrust the dolphin into the heavens, eternally surging as the constellation Delphinus.

As above, so below, for we have miniature versions of the marvelous creatures in our own gardens. Some poetic horticulturist noticed that the nectar cups of a plant resembled tiny dolphins leaping up the spike, and so named the lovely ruffled flower delphinium.

FROGS AND TOADS

FROGS and toads share a similar mythology, often negative, but toads fare even worse than frogs. Perhaps that is because frogs appear slightly more attractive to the human eye. Both are anurans, often aquatic, both have protruding eyes, webbed feet and large mouths, but frogs have smooth skins while toads tend to have squat, warty bodies. Frogs leap; toads flop along hop by awkward hop.

Down the ages frogs have inspired both repugnance and reverence. You might remember the fairy tale princess who kissed the frog and poof! A prince appeared. But in the original Grimm Brothers tale no kiss took place; the princess was revolted by the clammy croaker. She "flung him with all her might against the wall," and only then he became "a handsome prince with kind and grateful eyes."

Where frogs have aroused worship the watery creatures have been associated with rain, fertility and rebirth. Frog amulets have turned up in Egyptian tombs since the earliest dynasties, images of the goddess Heqet. Sometimes she was depicted as a frog, sometimes as a frog-headed woman, but always as "the Great Magician." Heqet represented the embryonic grain that seems to die, but then sends forth roots and sprouts. She lent her fertile presence when Isis had magical sexual union with the dead Osiris, god of resurrection, and

Heqet presided as midwife when god of the rising sun, Horus, was born of the outlandish coitus. In fact Heqet gave all Egyptians life, they believed, for at the original creation she touched lifeless humans with the ankh, breath filled their lungs and movement began. Like other birth goddesses she was a prophet, perhaps because the croaking of a frog was held to predict rain and the life-enhancing rising of the Nile.

The ancient Jews, on the other hand, abhorred frogs. In the book of Revelation, seven angels "pour out on the earth the seven bowls of the wrath of God." The sixth bowl contained "three foul spirits like frogs," demonic forces "performing signs." And in Exodus the creatures were summoned by Moses to effect the second plague of Egypt.

Frog beliefs leap from demonology to healing. In the classical Greek/Roman world a person suffering from infection of the left or right eye would hang the corresponding frog's eye around his neck for a cure. For toothache, the Greek physician Galen had the patient hold in his mouth a frog boiled in vinegar and water. A later Roman physician believed toothache could be cured by spitting in a frog's mouth and asking it to take the pain away.

The aquatic creatures often connect to the deluge myths found everywhere. In Australia the aborigines say that a vast frog once drank all the water in the world and caused great drought and misery. If they could only make the frog laugh, they reasoned, he would expel the water. Several of the animals cavorted about acting silly, but the unamused frog kept his huge mouth clamped. Then an eel wriggled in a giddy dance. The frog roared with laughter, and the water poured forth again to refresh the earth and restore life.

Early in America, frog beliefs tended to create positive magic. People believed that good luck followed if a frog entered your house or if you dreamed of frogs. Gamblers would win if they encountered a frog on their way to gaming. And killing a frog would make your cow's milk bloody.

As for their cousins the toads, mostly landlubbers, people everywhere considered them nasty. Although a boon to the garden, the creatures had an evil image, partly based on the milky venom they exude from their skin when excited or irritated. Toads often served as witches' familiars, and in some parts of Europe were believed to be witches themselves. Old conjuring books mention a potion of "toad milk and the sap of sow thistle" for nefarious purposes. The deadly substance secreted in toads' glands is identified by modern science as a powerful hallucinogen named "bufotenin" for the toad family.

A medieval legend about an "old and great toad" that bore a gemstone in its head inspired Renaissance jewelers. At a time when poisoning one's enemies was rampant, a so-called "toadstone" ring was prized as a forewarning. The gem was often an emerald or green agate reputed to be so sensitive as to lose its natural color in the presence of poison. Amber, coral, or ivory were other choices said to produce a warning heat when in contact with venom. Trust in the ring sprang from the assumption that since the toad carried poison, it also carried a means within itself to detect and counteract the effects. In *As You Like It* Shakespeare writes:

> *Sweet are the uses of adversity,*
> *Which, like the toad, ugly and venomous,*
> *Wears yet a precious jewel in his head.*

HARES
AND RABBITS

I shall go into a hare
With sorrow and sighing and mickle care,
And I shall go in the Devil's name
Till I come home again.

ITH THIS verse Isobell Gowdie revealed a shape-shifting secret in freely given testimony during her trial for witchcraft in 1662. The young Scottish witch regaled the court for four days with tales of her mystic adventures. A widely accepted view at the time was that a witch could by incantation actually become an animal. The hare along with cat and crow, magical creatures all, were favored forms of transformation. The belief that a witch while in the shape of a rabbit could only be killed by a silver bullet became part and parcel of British folklore.

Distinctions are few between hare and rabbit. Hares are larger and wilder than their rabbit kin, and the rabbit is more inclined to accept domestication. In lore and legend, however, the two are interchangeable. Both animals are prolific and flourish worldwide. In many cultures, past and present, hares and rabbits serve as fertility symbols.

Hares lead hounds and hunters a merry chase, swift when pursued and a marvel in zigzag coursing. Classical myths align the hare with fleet-of-foot Hermes, the messenger god and guide of the dead. An antique fable claims that Hermes placed the constellation Lepus, the Hare, in the heavens just out of range of Orion to annoy the mighty hunter.

Julius Caesar observed that Gauls held the hare sacred, and to hunt the animal or eat its flesh was forbidden. The ban was lifted only once a year on May Eve. The penalty for hunting hare at other times was to be struck with cowardice. The legendary British queen Boadicea, while leading a revolt against Roman rule, carried a hare into battle. She released it at a crucial moment in hope that the Romans would strike at it with their swords and thus lose courage. The taboo about eating rabbit persisted for centuries, due to fear that the animal's timid nature might be consumed as well.

In medieval Europe hares and rabbits acquired a reputation for mystery and magic. Their movements divined future events, and the unexpected sight of a hare or rabbit foreshadowed disaster. These creatures were, after all, allies of Hermes, the master magician, and companions of pagan woodland goddesses. Among the forty species of hares and rabbits, most choose to graze at twilight or at night. Nocturnal activity and kinship with the Moon alarmed the clergy.

In the East, from India to China, the hare and the Moon have close ties. Hindus see the hare's image on the Full Moon. The Buddha rewarded the hare with a place on the Moon, for it is said the creature leaped into a fire to save the holy man from starvation. According to Chinese legend, the Lunar Hare resides on the Moon under an acacia tree, where he pounds sacred herbs in a mortar to create the magical elixer of life.

In its own quiet way, the beautiful gentle hare/rabbit attained magical status. Perhaps that is why Lewis Carroll's Alice found Wonderland by following a white rabbit.

Alice's Adventures in Wonderland, Arthur Rackham, 1907

OWLS

THE BEHAVIOR of owls evokes dread. Their weird, melancholy call in an almost human voice shatters the still of the night. It may be followed by a blood-curdling shriek or a sound resembling mirthless laughter. The owl, with hunting skill that rivals the hawk's, is a nocturnal bird of prey with extraordinary hearing and keen eyesight. Its soft plumage assures silent flight ending in a swift kill. Owls choose to live in dark forests, thick pine groves, and deserted ruins. You will never see a flock of owls, for these creatures prefer a solitary existence. Mobs of other birds, especially crows, are ever ready to attack owls. From time to time, owls must seek refuge in hollow trees, abandoned nests, or caves. If encountered by day an owl shows no fear and may appear tame to the human intruder. However, its watchful stare and cool manner implies equality. The meeting may awaken thoughts of lost souls damned to live on as creatures of darkness and evil.

Owls live in all parts of the world and sinister themes permeate their lore and myth. A compelling tale is found in *The Mabinogion*, Welsh legends of the early Celtic world collected from oral tradition and written down in medieval times. Arianrod, mother of Llew, declared that her son should "never have a wife of the race that now inhabits this earth." Gwydion and Math, powerful magicians and protectors of Llew, were angered by Arianrod's prohibition and determined to thwart her will. By charms and illusion, they conjured a wife for Llew out of flowers. With blossoms of oak, broom, and meadowsweet, they produced a maiden, "the fairest and most graceful that man ever saw." They named her Blodeuwedd.

Llew and his bride prospered until one day in Llew's absence a young hunter appeared at Blodeuwedd's door. As soon as their eyes met, passion filled their hearts. Ardently declaring their love, the couple spent the evening rejoicing in its wonder. "Nor did they hesitate to embrace—and that night passed locked in each other's arms." The adulterous pair plotted to kill Llew. But Llew led a charmed life and could be slain only by a bizarre set of circumstances. Blodeuwedd, by deceitful means, secured the knowledge needed to do away with her husband, informed her lover, and arranged for the murder to take place. When Gwydion learned of Llew's fate, he vowed vengeance. Confronting Blodeuwedd, Gwydion said, "I will not slay thee, but I will do unto thee worse than that. For I will turn thee into a bird; and because of the shame thou hast done unto Llew, thou shalt never show thy face in the light of day henceforth; and that through fear of all other birds. For it shall be their nature to attack thee, and to chase thee wheresoever they may find thee."

On a cheerier note: ancient Egyptians designed a beautifully stylized owl, the hieroglyph representing the prepositions *in, from, of, at*—which explains the owl's frequent appearance on tomb and temple walls. The Greeks, bless them, chose the owl as Athena's bird. The goddess of wisdom endowed the bird with her own noble aspects.

SNAKES

SNAKES inspire more fear than esteem, and the dread goes beyond the fear of venom—most snakes are harmless. Death by snakebite is a rarity in America, but that doesn't lessen the mortal terror many people experience at the sudden sight of a wriggling snake. Jung pointed out that the snake represents the underworld and primordial matter, a prototype of the dark unknown, primitive, earthly, sinister. And the prevailing serpent myth of the Judaic-Christian world, its role as tempter in the Garden of Eden, hardly adds to its charm.

Yet some people are drawn to snakes, fascinated by their subtle beauty, grace, and swift, sinuous movement. Snakes slither the earth garbed in shining geometric patterns, natural Art Deco creatures; Shakespeare refers to their "enamell'd skin." Perhaps the snake lovers among us, long ago and in another incarnation, belonged to a culture that revered these strange footless reptiles. To the ancient Greeks and Romans, the snake's habit of sloughing its skin symbolized renewal. Hermes/Mercury, the messenger god and spirit guide of the underworld, carried a snake-entwined staff, the caduceus. Asclepius, the god of medicine, was also associated with snakes, and the caduceus became the insignia of the medical profession. The sight of a serpent was an omen of healing to the ill, a certain promise of returning vigor.

The Gnostic sects in Alexandria around the turn of the Christian era chose a snake holding its tail in its mouth, the ouroboros, to depict the reconciliation of opposites. This Western version of the Oriental yin and yang, half in light and half in darkness, denotes the potent phrase *en to pan*, all is one.

Serpent worship turns up in a surprisingly wide variety of myths and legends. Ancient Egyptian deities and rulers are crowned with the sacred snake symbol, the uraeus. Voodoo venerates the serpent Damballah as the oldest and primary divinity, and snakes play a beneficent role from Australian aborigines to Native American tribes. The snake conspicuously slithered its way into Toltec, Aztec and Maya pantheons, emerging as the creator-god. They knew it as Quetzalcoatl, the plumed serpent, every coil covered in spectacular emerald-green feathers, god of wind, wisdom and life. Although the snake is often identified with underworld aspects, it is also associated with rainbows linking heaven and earth.

But despite such exalted roles elsewhere, for many people the glimpse of a curling snake evokes the same eerie feeling as Emily Dickinson voices:

Several of nature's people
I know, and they know me;
I feel for them a transport
Of cordiality;

But never met this fellow,
Attended or alone,
Without a tighter breathing,
And zero at the bone.

SPIDERS

THE SPIDER is commonly maligned. "Do you realize that if I didn't catch bugs and eat them, bugs would increase and multiply and get so numerous that they'd destroy the earth, wipe out everything?" The wise spider with the sweetly musical voice in E.B. White's *Charlotte's Web* is not just spinning a tale. She is ecologically correct. And when people spot one of her relatives in the house, what thanks do they generally offer? Brisk dispatch.

Several unsound reasons may exist for such antipathy. Humankind tends to feel uneasy about black creatures that move swiftly and silently. Spiders live alone, preferring solitude to the bustle of community life, and loners are often viewed with suspicion in our gregarious culture. Mostly we fear the bite of spiders, but these are seldom if ever fatal. The creatures do have one distressing trait by human standards;

the male always dies after mating, sometimes from the bite of the female, sometimes from sheer exhaustion.

Spiders are not insects but with scorpions are classified as *Arachnida*, named for a great weaver in an ancient tale. Arachne was so proud of her work that she boasted it was more beautiful than the cloth Minerva wove. The goddess, who clothed in splendor all the deities on Mount Olympus, was outraged at the peasant girl's audacity and challenged her to a contest. Both set to their looms in Arachne's forest hut and their shuttles flew. According to the mythologist Edith Hamilton: "Minerva did her best and the result was a marvel, but Arachne's work, finished at the same moment, was in no way inferior. The goddess in a fury of anger slit the web from top to bottom and beat the girl around the head with her shuttle. Arachne, disgraced and mortified and furiously angry, hanged herself. Then a little repentance entered Minerva's heart. She lifted the body from the noose and sprinkled it with a magic liquid. Arachne was changed into a spider, and her skill in weaving was left to her."

As if to right a serious wrong toward spiders, many societies have held the spider to be lucky. The Greeks and Romans believed a spider engraved on a precious stone conferred foresight on one who wore it. According to Celtic lore, seeing a spider spinning is an omen that good fortune is near. And killing a spider in Britain was thought to bring on a long spell of rain. Confining a spider in a walnut shell to wear around the neck as a cure for ailments was as popular in the 18th century as when the ancient Greeks wore the same odd pendants.

Spiders are superb engineers. To watch a beautifully symmetrical web emerge from the hectic dance of the spider is fascinating—and in one historical instance inspiring. After a number of defeats against Britain, the Scottish liberator Robert the Bruce hid in a cave, vanquished and miserable. Looking up he sighted a spider attempting to anchor its web. Six times it failed, but the seventh try was successful. Taking such tenacity as a sign, the future king determined never to give up until he prevailed.

In 17th-century England Mirabel Bedford, an accused witch, kept a spider as a familiar and addressed it as Joan. Witches to this day hold a tender regard for the marvel of spiders and allow webs house room, holding to the old couplet:

If you wish to live and thrive, let a spider run alive.

SWANS

SWANS belong to northern climes, the place viewed by ancient people as mysterious and magical. Breeding in the northernmost area of their range, swans wing south to winter in Europe, China, Japan, and the United States. Their great size and bright white plumage stirred the imagination. Swans gliding smoothly, silently on water were a sight of striking beauty and grace. The splendid visitors inspired myths for as long as there have been mythmakers.

A Native American legend of the Blackfoot tribe depicts swans as helpers in a hero's quest to visit the Sun. After a series of adventures, the youth faces a great expanse of water separating him from his goal. A hopeless feeling envelops him and then: "Two swans came swimming. They asked him who he was and what had brought him to that shore. He responded, and they said, 'Take heart. Across this water is the lodge of that

Person Above whom you seek. Get on our backs, and we shall take you there.' He waded in, lay on their backs, and they started. Very deep and black is that water. Strange beings inhabit it: monsters that seize people and drown them. Yet the two swans carried him safely to the other shore, where a broad trail led from the water. 'Hyi!' said the swans. 'Follow that trail.'"

Another tale concerns transition and is the source of the expression "swan song" to describe a final performance. The story derives from Finland's ancient epic poem, the *Kalevala*. Sibelius, the eminent Finnish composer, reflects the atmosphere of this runic legend in his hauntingly beautiful tone poem, "Swan of Tuonela." Tuonela, the land of death, is a dark underground kingdom ringed by a black river upon which a majestic swan glides. The swan's song is a plaintive melody, and whoever hears it must leave the reality of this world and venture into a strange, unknown land. The swan represents a spirit guide as the soul passes from one place to another.

Swan transformation myths are a recurrent theme in literature and other arts, from the tragic Irish tale, *Children of Lir*, to *Lohengrin*, the operatic Swan Knight of German lore, to the Russian tale of *Swan Lake*, basis of the lovely ballet.

Zeus, sky god of the Greeks, chose the guise of a swan in order to seduce Leda, queen of twilight. Their coupling produced two eggs. From the first came Castor and Pollux, the heavenly twins, and the second held Clytemnestra and the ill-fated Helen of Troy. Some scholars say Leda's spouse Tyndareus fathered one set of twins, but authorities differ over which egg was which. The myth inspired many painters, especially during the Renaissance, and most major museums possess a version of

Leda and the Swan. The poet Yeats wrote a superb account of the seduction: "A sudden blow: the great wings beating still above the staggering girl…"

Apollo, Greek god of music and poetry, was linked to the bird, for it was believed that his soul passed into a swan. From this legend arose the tradition that the souls of all good poets live on as swans. Ben Jonson called Shakespeare the "Swan of Avon." Not only poets are affiliated with swans. Diogenes Laertius in his *Lives of Eminent Philosophers*, third century CE, wrote: "Socrates in a dream saw a cygnet on his knees, which all at once put forth plumage, and flew away after uttering a loud sweet note. And the next day Plato was introduced as a pupil, and Socrates recognized him as the swan of his dream."

Fabulous
Creatures

If there have been, are and always will be,
more things in heaven and earth than were
dreamed of in Horatio's philosophy, we must
understand that one of the channels which led
to the creation of fabulous animals was pure fact.

—T.H. WHITE

BASILISK

BEWARE the basilisk unless, of course, you are carrying a weasel in a cage. Without such protection the beast can slay you in unpleasant ways. It is the Evil Eye made manifest, capable of "looking anyone dead." The range of the monster's fiery glance is so far-reaching that it can make a lark flying past plummet from the air, deliciously fried, into the gaping mouth. Where the monster roams becomes the bleakest of deserts. Nothing survives, for its visual venom blackens grass, rots the fruits of the earth and even splits rocks. Where the basilisk simply happens by, water turns toxic.

Sometimes called a cockatrice, the basilisk has the body of a large snake with the head and legs of a cock, wide thorny wings, and a tail ending in a hook or arrowpoint. Two stories prevail about the birth of the sinister creature. One tells us that it sprang from a round yolkless egg laid by a seven-year-old

Basilisk, Nuremberg, 1510

rooster and hatched by a toad. The other reveals that the
basilisk is the offspring of the Gorgon Medusa, whose glance
turned living beings into stone and from whose jaws "snakes
poured forth whizzing hisses with vibrating tongues, which,
after the manner of a woman's hair flowing along the back,

flapped about the very neck of the delighted Medusa. Upon her forehead turned towards you erect did serpents rise, and viper's venom flowed from her combed locks."

The basilisk's stare was so potent that a hunter raising a spear to the beast was slain as the poison flowed up the weapon and into the man's heart—also killing the horse upon which he was mounted.

The monster's name derives from the Greek term meaning "little king," for the ancients regarded the basilisk as the king of serpents. The creature's original aspect sprang from that of a cobralike snake, and over time the image of the crest on the head evolved into a cockscomb, perceived in legend as a crown. But through all its evolutions the basilisk's nature has always been considered dire, for snakes have had a bad press long before Genesis.

You may be wondering about the weasel. The ancient warning actually refers to the mongoose, a fierce little ferret notable in India for its aptitude in killing cobras. It performs the same service with basilisks, for on spotting a mongoose the basilisk turns its slithery tail and runs off. Should a mongoose not be handy when you encounter a basilisk, a mirror offers equal protection—if the creature sees its own image, it dies of fright.

In the 17th century, literal belief in the monster began to wane. The Spanish poet Quevedo wrote the beautifully logical, beautifully mocking lines about the basilisk: "If the man who saw you is still alive, / Your whole story is a lie, / Since if he has not died he cannot have seen you, / And if he has died, he cannot tell what he saw."

CENTAURS

AN from head to torso, horse from torso south, centaurs canter along in the retinue of Dionysus, celebrating the rites and delights of the vine with Pan, Silenus, Eros, satyrs, nymphs and bacchantes. Like other rural divinities centaurs are gross brutes, prone to lechery and drunkenness. They are the offspring of Ixion, a Greek mortal, and a cloud, yes, a cloud, begotten in this bizarre fashion: Hot-headed Ixion quarreled with his future father-in-law and killed him. Pursued for the murder, he prayed to Zeus for salvation so earnestly that the god granted him refuge on Mount Olympus. Ixion repaid the hospitality by attempting to seduce Hera, the wife of Zeus and queen of heaven itself. To test the ingrate's audacity, Zeus formed a cloud in the tempting shape of Hera, and Ixion promptly coupled with the beautiful goddess-who-wasn't-there. Further enraged, Zeus caused a monster to be born of the misty union. Centaurus, the beast created by the lust of Ixion and the malice of Zeus, mated with the mares of Thessaly and fathered the raunchy race of centaurs.

Enormously fond of horses, Greeks were unafraid of centaurs and relished their company in some tales. But on one notorious occasion their bestial behavior led to a full-scale battle. Invited to attend the wedding of the King of Thessaly, the carousing centaurs got so drunk that they attempted to ravish the women, including the bride. A brawl followed, with slaughter on both sides. Finally the centaurs galloped off, but returned later with allies armed with big rocks and uprooted pine trees. Despite the heavy rural artillery the centaurs were defeated, and the battle marked the last friendship between mankind and the centaurs.

The exception was Chiron, educated by Apollo and Artemis, granted wisdom and eternal life. He was the mentor of Greek heroes, including Achilles and Jason, each of whom served an apprenticeship in the wilderness with the centaur. And Chiron is also singular for ceding immortality. Accidentally shot with a magical poisoned arrow by his friend Heracles, the centaur preferred death to unending pain and passed his gift of everlasting life to the fire-giver Prometheus. Yet Chiron is still poetically eternal. Zeus thrust the image of the noble centaur into the heavens, where he may be seen wheeling the night skies as the constellation Sagittarius the Archer.

CHIMERA

HIMERA is another Greek mythological animal you don't want to chance meeting, not even in your dreams. The beast would be easy enough to recognize, having the head of a lion, the torso of a goat, and the tail of a serpent. Sometimes the chimera, a female, is depicted as having three heads—a snake's head springs from the tail and a goat's head springs from the body, in addition to the fierce frontal lion. To make the "mingled monster" even more unprepossessing, the chimera has a fiery breath that sizzles to a crisp anything within range except the odd hero. Homer tells us that "Her pitchy nostrils flaky flames expire; / Her gaping throat emits infernal fire."

The beast may have been a metaphor for her birthplace in Lycia, where a volcano is called the Chimera. Serpents pervade the base of the mountain, goats graze on the meadows above, and lions were rumored to lurk toward the arid top, which belched flames. Since lions do not actually inhabit Greece, and since no one had actually ever seen a chimera, at some point doubt began to arise as to the creature's actual existence. The skepticism led to the modern definition of a chimera, "a vain or foolish fancy."

But before disbelief more or less erased the chimera from zoology, a tale evolved of its slaying. The hero was Bellerophon, a young prince who had fallen under the spell of Philonoe, the princess of Lycia. Reluctant to part with his daughter, King

Chimera, Etruscan bronze, 5th century BCE

Iobates dispatched Bellerophon to kill the chimera, certain that the unwelcome suitor would perish in flames. But the goddess Athena, inventor of the bridle and tamer of horses, took pity on the handsome prince. She presented him with a golden bridle and revealed how to capture milk-white Pegasus, winged steed of the gods. "He will help you win the battle," she promised.

At the fountain of Hippocrene, the prince threw the bridle over the horse's head and thrust the golden bit between his teeth. Immediately tamed by Athena's magic, the horse soared up with the mounted Bellerophon in search of the chimera. Guided by the stench of burning greenery, Pegasus swooped from the sky so swiftly and Bellerophon dealt such mighty blows that the monster finally lay lifeless, her power destroyed. In Lycia the deed was celebrated with much rejoicing and a royal wedding.

The tale enriches us with its whiff of the heroic—and with "chimerical," a useful word to evoke when we set off in hot pursuit of a foolish dream.

DRAGONS

O F ALL fabulous beasts, the dragon has found its way into the most legends. Everyone is familiar with the monster's image—a scaly serpentine body and tail, large batlike wings, stumpy legs with claws, glaring eyes, and a fang-rimmed mouth emitting flames and smoke. The creature's formidable appearance beautifully fits the archetype, for in Western mythology the dragon personifies wickedness. It is the antithesis of the hero, their battles the symbolic clash of good and evil.

The successful dragon-slayer risks his life but shines his way down through history. Similar stories abound. A dragon captures a beautiful virgin, usually royal, and usually binds her to a rock. A knight contends for her release, slays the monster and gets to wed the princess. St. George is perhaps the most notable dragon hero. In this tale from the Middle Ages, every year a maiden had to be sacrificed to prevent the beast from laying waste to the

St. George slays the dragon, Albrecht Dürer, 1505

countryside. The year that the lot fell to the Princess Sabra, she was rescued by this dauntless champion of Christendom. St. George slew the beast with one blow of his magic sword Ascalon, and by the deed not only won the princess but won the town over to Christianity. In earlier Greek mythology the valiant Perseus fared the same with the same elements—the beautiful princess Andromeda chained to a cliff, a monster slain by a sword, an acclaimed hero, a wedding, an enduring romantic tale.

Early cultures had a literal belief in the existence of dragons, and the Romans had some odd ideas about their behavior. According to the historian Pliny, Ethiopian dragons in search of more hospitable climates often navigated the Red Sea to Arabia. To make the crossing, four or five dragons coiled together to form a boat, pumping their powerful legs, their heads swaying above the water. Pliny also devotes a chapter to remedies and benefits derived from slain dragons. He assures us that their eyes, dried and stirred with honey, make a potion to prevent nightmares; that a litigant will win his case if dragon-heart fat is daubed on a gazelle hide and bound to the arm with sinews of a stag; dragon teeth, also tied to the body, assure the lenience of masters and the mercy of kings.

Despite its fiery breath, the dragon's mythological element is water rather than fire. It chooses to dwell in watery or misty caves, often as a guardian of treasure. In Teutonic mythology the dragon Fafnir lurks in a cave and keeps a hoard with occult powers. Siegfried slays the monster, the tale immortalized at stunning length in the Wagnerian operas.

But in the East, especially in China, people love dragons. A Dragon Year, which ushered in the new millennium, portends riches and harmony, and at New Year's vivid dragons are pranced through streets in Chinese communities all over the world. The creatures are believed to be the givers of laws, fertility, swords, painting and magic. In art, clouds issue from their mouths rather than fire. As beings of splendor dragons once flew on the nation's flag and are associated with the possessions of emperors: the dragon throne, the dragon boat, the dragon bed, and so on.

In the words of Jorge Luis Borges, "There is something in the dragon's image that fits man's imagination."

GRIFFINS

THE GRIFFIN is a rarity, doubly royal. The creature has the head and wings of an eagle, king of birds, and the body of a lion, king of beasts; it is symbolically potent for dominion over earth and sky. Griffins are notable for their strength and intelligence, and an old text assures us that they are the size of eight lions and have the strength of one hundred eagles. A griffin can "bear to his nest flying a horse and a man upon his back or two oxen yoked together as they go at plow." The concept of mighty eagle-lions arose in the Middle East, and they often turn up in the art of the ancient Babylonians, Assyrians and Persians.

As befits royalty, griffins love anything that glitters, especially gold. They have the ability to sense buried treasure, and atop the trove they build nests of gold and lay eggs of agate. Many a missing jewel might have been found in the cache of a griffin high in a mountain aerie. They defend their riches against all possible plunderers, and griffins became notable as ferocious guardians of precious things, both their own and those of emperors and gods. The ancient Greeks believed that griffins, the duality both sun creatures, drew the golden chariot of the sun god Apollo across the sky each day. Alexander the Great yearned for his own griffin to fly him to the edge of the sky. Nemesis, goddess of retribution, held griffins sacred and sometimes called upon their services to enact revenge. But in its most noble portrayal, valiant and forbidding, the griffin emerged during the Middle Ages as a key figure in heraldry. It arises rampant on the coats of arms and banners of kings,

Gryphon fast asleep, Sir John Tenniel, 1865

generals, aristocrats—in "wakeful custody," balanced on one or two lion paws, ready to strike with talons. Fierce images of griffins often loom from Gothic churches as gargoyles, in earlier versions created to scare demons or avert evil, in later architecture mainly ornamental.

Griffins had no particular enmity for people, but they dispatched dragons, snakes and horses, although they sometimes mated with mares. Their progeny were hippogriffs, an odd assemblage of feathered flying horses.

The most famous griffin, superstar of the species, bumbles its delightful way through the pages of Lewis Carroll's *Alice in Wonderland*. A surrealistic punster, the Gryphon informs Alice that he studied with a classical master and learned Laughing and Grief.

"And how many hours a day did you do lessons?" asked Alice.

"Ten hours the first day; nine the next; and so on."

"What a curious plan!" exclaimed Alice.

"That's the reason they're called lessons," the Gryphon remarked, "because they lessen from day to day."

PHOENIX

MOST creatures spring from other creatures. But there is only one phoenix ranging the sky, and this rarest of birds clones itself everlastingly from the burned bones of its own body. When it has divided the air for five hundred years and its wings falter, the phoenix builds itself a nest atop an Arabian date palm tree. In this tree it collects cinnamon, spikenard and myrrh, and of those splendid materials builds a heap on which to enact its fiery perfumed death.

The nest of leaves and bark becomes both grave and cradle.

Here the bird flutters its wings so rapidly that sparks glitter among feathers, and in this way flames begin snapping from beak to claws. The dying bird sings so melodiously, so gloriously, that winged creatures throng from skies everywhere to marvel. The phoenix expires singing its incomparable dirge in a sphere of spicy sweetness.

Phoenix, Basle, 1557

A worm humps its way out of the ashes. From this small-ness and smoothness a young phoenix emerges nine days later. Some ancient myths tell us that the bird was crimson and gold and resembled an eagle; other legends claim that it was purple and resembled a heron; all agree that it was a creature of unsur-passed beauty.

Its first act is to pat together a little egg of its own charred remains mixed with myrrh. With the egg in its beak, the phoenix flies to Heliopolis, the City of Sun on the Nile Delta. It is accompanied by a throng of birds and more join in flight. And in Egypt, every five hundred years, the phoenix was welcomed by high ritual in the Temple of Atum-Ra. The bird deposited its father-self egg on the pyramidal summit of the sacred obelisk and swooped out to begin its cycle anew.

Alchemists chose the phoenix as their symbol and early chemists were located by the sign of the phoenix swinging above the door. The Old Testament mentions the bird in Job, and Christian monks who wrote medieval bestiaries took the phoenix as a point of departure for a scolding: "If the Phoenix has the power to die and rise again, why, silly man, are you scandalized at the word of God."

Beginning with the Renaissance and early scientific observation, the phoenix vanished from bestiaries. But the bird has never migrated from poetry. Since antiquity the phoenix has burned brightly in the hearts of poets, both as immortality symbol and as exotic legend. None wrote more beautifully about the bird than John Dryden:

> *So when the new-born Phoenix first is seen*
> *Her feathered subjects all adore their queen,*
> *And while she makes progress through the East,*
> *From every grove her numerous train's increased;*
> *Each poet of the air her glory sings,*
> *And round him the pleased audience clap their wings.*

SALAMANDER

THE ZOOLOGICAL salamander is an unremarkable little amphibian that resembles a lizard. But its mythological counterpart has a uniquely wondrous quality — a body so icy that it can withstand flames.

Numerous old stories attest to such sightings, including one by the Renaissance artist Cellini documented in his autobiography. At age five, gazing into a log fire, he spotted a little creature weaving its head, waving its tail and frolicking in the flames. Excitedly he called his father to witness the spectacle. The father, equally amazed, soundly smacked the boy's ear to assure that the child would remember the scene forever. The act was a deplorable memory aid, but Signor Cellini believed that they were seeing a sight granted few humans — a magical little dragon.

Belief concerning the salamander's marvelous virtue existed in ancient Egypt and Babylon. In Greece, Aristotle wrote that

Salamander, Frankfurt, 1687

the salamander "not only walks through fire, but puts it out in doing so." Roman naturalist Pliny described the creature as "so intensely cold as to extinguish fire by its contact, in the same way that ice does." A medieval monk kept the myth alive by recording: "This animal is the only one which puts the flames out. Indeed, it lives in the middle of the blaze without being hurt and without being burnt." The scholarly monarch Francis I of

FABULOUS CREATURES

France chose as his emblem a salamander in flames with the motto: "I nourish and extinguish."

But the mythical lizard gained enduring magical significance in the Renaissance, when Paracelsus, the great Swiss magus, declared the salamander to be the Elemental of Fire. The doctrine of Paracelsus held that Elementals were primal beings inhabiting the classical four roots of matter: gnomes of Earth, sylphs of Air, and undines of Water. The salamander of Fire symbolically expressed a spark igniting action, purification, and transformation. Paracelsus equated the essence of fire with the power of imagination in the human spirit: "that explosive flare that lights up the inner spaces, revealing meaning."

No great leap of imagination is required to guess the origin of the fabulous salamander, given the zoological creature's actual habits. The tiny lizard likes to cozy up in a log with a nice damp hole. And if such a log turns up in a fireplace and the salamander is rudely awakened by flames, its movements are less frolic than frantic, a usually successful scramble for life. Young Cellini undoubtedly reported what he saw correctly and took a blow to remember the fiery little dragon surviving despite all odds. The memory served Cellini well, for he managed to keep a cool head in a hotbed of court intrigues, all the while producing beautiful art in his wild and wonderful career.

SELKIES

BELOW the chilly waters of the Shetland and Orkney Islands lived the Selkies, strange seal people who inhabited a netherworld below the depths of the sea. They were fallen angels, the Scots believed, banished to the sea for their sins but allowed human form on dry land. They enjoyed donning sealskins from head to toe and swimming upward from one region of air to another, where they shed their soft fur and sometimes pleasantly encountered mortals.

The strange creatures were extraordinarily beautiful, as befits angels, and women became wildly enchanted by Selkie men at a glance. The amorous seal creatures enjoyed making love to human women and made expeditions to that purpose, but seldom stayed long. Male Selkies tended to seduce and abandon, even as some mortal counterparts. But Ursilla, a passionate island woman, kept one close for years. Discontented with her fisherman husband, she invoked a Selkie by sitting on a rock at high tide and dropping seven tears into the sea. A lover duly arrived and returned often enough to father numerous offspring, all of whom had webbed hands and feet.

Selkie women had a different story. They loved dancing as much as their cousins the mermaids loved singing, shedding their sealskins and cavorting nude on beaches. The divinely graceful dancer with pearly skin, legs flashing and golden hair flying, was a riveting sight for mortal man, set immediately

aflame with desire. The island men had learned that if they stole the sealskin and hid it, the beauty became a reluctant captive—but would nonetheless serve as a fond but somewhat sad wife and mother. She would roam the beaches at high tide during the Full Moon, all dance vanished from her limbs, nostalgic for her undersea realm and Selkie husband. She never stopped searching for the sealskin, and if she found the hidden fur she would slip it on and streak downward to reunite with her first love, her true love. And that is probably as things should be.

Mermaids and Selkies have a great mutual tenderness nurtured through an ancient myth: A young fisherman had stunned and skinned a Selkie, throwing her body into the water and pretending to the other fishermen that he had found a dead seal. But the Selkie was still alive, although gravely injured, and regained consciousness in the sea. Cold and pitiful, she found her way into an underwater cave inhabited by a mermaid. Touched by the plight of the Selkie, the mermaid swam upward to try regaining the Selkie's sealskin. In the boat where the sealskin lay she permitted herself to be caught in the net, to the stupefaction of the crew. Remorseful at his destruction of the Selkie the young fisherman tried to free the mermaid, but the others were determined to take the rarity ashore and sell this most valuable of finny creatures.

The poor mermaid, still tangled in the lines, was laid on the sealskin and the boat sped toward shore. But mermaids cannot long endure the upper air, and her life was ebbing. She knew that Selkie men would exact revenge by sending a gale and sinking the ship. The mermaid's last wish was that the skin would sink with her body down to the cave. That is how it happened. The Selkie, grieving for her brave friend, slipped on her sealskin, revived shortly and dove down, down to her natural element.

Since that time Selkies have been loving toward mermaids, and will risk their lives to provide them protection.

How do we know this? Perhaps a mermaid sang the tale to a mortal who passed it down.

UNICORNS

O F ALL the creatures in the Zoo of the Fabulous, the unicorn is perhaps the most beautiful. It is a horse slightly larger than the real thing, perfectly formed on its slim legs, eyes blue as sapphires, from its forehead arising a long horn with a red tip like a little flame. The unicorn ambles its way through the forest, a flash of gleaming white amid the greenery.

But such glamour is a modern concept. In its mythological onset the unicorn is an outlandish creature as described by the Roman naturalist Pliny. He assures us that it is "similar in the rest of its body to a horse, with the head of a deer, the feet of an elephant, the tail of a boar." It is a "very ferocious beast," he says, and cannot be taken alive. Perhaps that explained to the populace why unicorns found no place in the Coliseum among the thousands of lions, panthers and rhinos slaughtered in lethal entertainments. The Chinese also recognized the unicorn as an odd assembly of body parts, calling it "the four-not-like"—the body of a horse but not like a horse, the feet of an antelope but not like an antelope, the head of a deer but not like a deer, the tail of a boar but not like a boar.

Hunters considered unicorns prize game, but were sorely puzzled about how to overcome such fierce creatures. They believed that the horn functioned like a small sword, movable at the animal's will, and only a fine fencer could survive the bizarre duel. Others maintained that the sword had magical strength, and that the pursued unicorn could throw itself over a cliff, land on its horn, and canter away unscathed. During the Middle Ages, the myth spins off in another fanciful direction. The unicorn was a great lover of purity, it was believed, and powerfully attracted to virginal innocence. Hunters began taking to the field with maidens, who would sit in conspicuous sites. When the unicorn spied the girl, it would approach with all reverence, lay its head gently on her lap and fall asleep. The treacherous maiden would then signal hunters, who would seize the beast. Artists loved the visual appeal of the story, and the unicorn hunt turns up in widespread medieval works from Europe, the Islamic world and China.

Throughout the ages and shifting stories people believed that the horn had magical properties. Dipping a horn into water purified the drink. Stomach trouble and epilepsy vanished at a swig of unicorn-horn elixir. Medieval kings and popes owned unicorn horns and used them as amulets to detect poisons in their food. As late as the 16th century the horns were used as very expensive antidotes.

By about that time belief in the unicorn dwindles and disappears, although in 1673 a Dr. Olfert Dapper reports spotting one in the Maine woods. And a unicorn turns up in the Lewis Carroll children's classic. At their encounter Alice says, "Do you know, I always thought unicorns were fabulous monsters. I never saw one alive before!"

"Well, now that we have seen each other," said the Unicorn, "if you'll believe in me, I'll believe in you. Is that a bargain?"

"Yes, if you like," said Alice. And that seems fair enough.

Magic Storied Creatures

Animals are stylized characters in a kind of old
saga – stylized because even the most acute of
them have little leeway as they play out their parts

— EDWARD HOAGLAND, in *Heart's Desire*

THE BEASTS OF BORGES

I N 1957 Jorge Luis Borges, the superb Argentinian poet, published the *Manual de Zoología Fantástica*. A later English edition, the *Book of Imaginary Beings*, created with translator Norman Thomas di Giovanni, contains descriptions of 120 mythical beasts from folklore and literature. There follow some of our favorites.

In the preface, Borges states that the book is to be read "as with all miscellanies not straight through. Rather we would like the reader to dip into the pages at random, just as one plays with the shifting patterns of a kaleidoscope."

Á Bao a Qu — A creature that lives on the staircase of the Tower of Victory in Chitor. It may only move when a traveler climbs the staircase, and it follows close at the person's heels. Its form becomes more complete the closer it gets to the terrace at the tower's top. It can only achieve this ultimate form if the traveler has obtained Nirvana, otherwise it finds itself unable to continue.

Animals in the Form of Spheres — At the time of its writing, some believed that planets and stars were actually living beings and that the movement of the heavenly bodies was voluntary.

Antelopes with Six Legs — According to Siberian myth, these six-legged antelopes were far too fast for human beings to catch. A divine huntsman, Tunk-poj, cut off the animal's rear-most legs to make the animal easier for humans to hunt.

The Ass with Three Legs — This massive creature is said to stand in the middle of the ocean. It has three legs, six eyes, nine mouths, and one golden horn.

Bahamut — A huge, measureless fish which is often used to describe the spaces between heaven, earth, and hell.

Catoblepas — Described as a black buffalo with a hog's head, this creature's head is so heavy that it constantly hangs low to the ground. It is also believed that, like the basilisk, looking into its eyes will kill you instantly.

Celestial Stag—No one has ever seen a Celestial Stag. They live in underground mines, searching for the light of day. They will attempt to bribe, speak to, and even torture miners in their quest to reach the surface, where they turn into a deadly liquid form.

The Chinese Fox—These foxes appear like average foxes, but may sometimes be seen standing on their hind legs to walk. They presumably live about a thousand years, and are bad omens for their mischievous ways. They are known to shapeshift and are able to see into the future.

Eater of the Dead—Most commonly associated with Egyptian myth, the Eater attends to the "wicked." It is described as having the head of a crocodile, the midsection of a lion, and the hindquarters of a hippo.

Eight-Forked Serpent—A massive serpent with eight heads and eight tails. Its eyes are a deep red, and trees are said to grow along its back.

The Elephant That Foretold the Birth of the Buddha—A white elephant with six tusks that appeared in a dream to, as its namesake suggests, foretell the birth of Buddha.

The Wonders of God's Creation Manifested in the Variety of Eight—A mysterious creature that lives in the world of

Bliss. Allegedly, all sounds, sights, and smells to this creature are divine.

Fastitocalon—A massive whale that many sailors often mistake for an island.

Fauna of Mirrors—It was believed that another world existed behind all mirrors, inhabited by a wide amount of unknown and strange creatures. Luckily, our worlds are now cut off from one another.

Gillygaloo—A bird which nests on mountain slopes and lays square eggs, which lumberjacks use as dice.

Goofang—A fish ("about the size of a sunfish but much bigger") which swims backwards to keep the water out of its eyes.

Goofus Bird—A bird that builds its nest upside down and flies backwards.

Huallepen—A swift-moving dog with a human head, which laughs maliciously.

Hundred-Heads—The Hundred-Heads was said to be a gigantic fish with many heads, each one that of a different animal. Legend holds that the fish was the reincarnated spirit of a monk who had often called others "monkey-head" or something similar. The karma of these insults had made him return as a monster.

THE BEASTS OF BORGES

The Lamed Wufniks — There are precisely thirty-six Lamed Wufniks in existence. It is said that, without knowing it, they support the universe and affirm god. If one comes to realize their purpose, they immediately die and are replaced by another unsuspecting man.

Lamia — Half woman and half serpent, these creatures are said to have sprung from one of Zeus's varied love interests. They are thought to be sorceresses, and although they cannot speak they whistle sweetly.

The Leveler — Reputed to live on the planet Neptune, this creature is ten times the size of an elephant, and looks quite a bit like it. Its most remarkable features are its conical legs (which are flat on the bottom). Bricklayers employ the Leveler to flatten hilly areas for construction projects. It is herbivorous and has few enemies.

The Monkey of the Inkpot — an extract from *Wang Tai-Hai* describes a small creature with black fur and scarlet eyes that sits by writers and drinks their leftover ink.

The Mother of Tortoises — A giant tortoise made of water and fire, on whose shell is written the "Universal Rule," a divine treatise.

Ping Feng — A black pig with a head at each end.

Pinnacle Grouse — Has only one wing, and flies in a continuous circle around the top of a mountain.

Strong Toad — Distinguished from other toads by its turtle-like shell, the Strong Toad glows like a firefly, cannot be killed except by burning, and can attract or repel anyone nearby with its stare.

Swedenborg's Angels — The perfected souls of the blessed and wise, living in a Heaven of ideal things, each reflecting the perfection of this realm.

Swedenborg's Devils — These are people which, after dying, choose to go to hell rather than to heaven. They are not happy there, but they are reputed to be more content in hell than they would have been in heaven.

The T'ao T'ieh — a dog with one (often monstrous) head attached to two bodies, which symbolizes the sins of gluttony and greed.

BRIAN BORU'S POOKA HORSE

THE ANCIENT High King of Ireland, renowned for bravery, experienced a ride on a ferocious pooka horse. Brian Boru risked breaking his royal neck to capture the beast, a destroyer of the realm's farms. The king drew three hairs from its tail, and wove them into a magic bridle. Astride the pooka a mighty combat began, horse vs. man, each power determined to prevail. The horse bucked, kicked, vaulted, heaved, yanked the bridle, swivelled its head to bite. Brian Boru hung on for hours until the horse exhausted itself, and finally the rider assumed control. Like other pookas, the horse had the power of speech. The king extracted two promises: It would never again vandalize property and never again harm any Irishmen except those that were drunk or "abroad with evil intent." The latter were fair game and could be assaulted even more fiercely than before. But who can trust the word of a horse? Over the years the pooka seems to have broken its promise, for attacks on property and sober travelers are said to continue down to this day.

THE
CALICO CAT
FURRY COLLAGE OF CONUNDRUMS

CALICO CATS have long enjoyed a connection with the weird and off beat. The dignified tuxedo cat; the legendary status of luck and magic enjoyed by felines of pure white or black; the playful tiger stripes and Garfield-like confidence of the orange marmalade—all are dear to cat fanciers. However none of these can match the eccentric mix in both temperament and appearance of the calico.

A kitty with a coat of at least three different colors, calicos are almost always female. They can resemble a furry crazy-patch quilt covered with random splotches of orange, black, white and even brown or gray. Sometimes the effect is truly ugly. In other cases a calico will have a unique beauty all its own. Beautiful or grotesque, the calico cat's outer appearance of confusion reflects the inner personality and psyche. Its behavior is crazed to the point that many observers are convinced that the cat is truly insane. Perhaps this gives rise to the ill omens linked to calicos. Some years ago U.S. Attorney General John Ashcroft reportedly became agitated when he spotted a calico cat watching him. The incident occurred outside Ashcroft's hotel in The Netherlands just before an important meeting. He was certain that the cat was a harbinger of impending chaos.

The term calico cat was adopted from the name of a whimsical fabric. In earlier times printed cotton cloth was called calico. Colorful, casual and comfortable, it provided an alternative to the more formal and expensive linens, wools and silks. Perhaps the name provides the clue to understanding and appreciating the unique spirit of the calico. Individual, unpredictable and interesting, the calico cat is in harmony with the human urge to relax and be ourselves, oblivious to the demands and expectations of the rest of the world.

— DIKKI-JO MULLEN

121

TWO BEARS SOAR SKYWARD

CALLISTO sprang from a strange father, himself a victim of metamorphosis. Lycaon, the king of Arcadia, had been changed into a wolf because of blasphemy: he had invited Zeus to his home and set a dish of human flesh before the god. Now Lycaon ran with wolves on four bony legs, his punishment deserved. But his lovely daughter Callisto also was transformed onto a beast, innocent as a lamb though she was.

Callisto followed in the retinue of Artemis, goddess of female virginity, who also manifested as a huntress roving fields and woods. Of all the huntresses following Artemis her favorite was Callisto, the Beautiful One. She had held up her vow of chastity faithfully, but she reckoned without Zeus. The strong huntress fought him off, terrified of violating the vow that defined her life. But Zeus made love to Callisto even as they struggled. He then flew skyward, leaving his victim dazed on the grass.

Soon her swollen body was visible proof of the sacrilege violating the oath that defined the cult. She was too ashamed to explain. Artemis swore revenge, but she would bide her time until Callisto's child would be delivered. The goddess struck immediately after childbirth, turning Callisto into a bear. Zeus snatched the infant and flew skyward. The god named his godling Arcas after Arcadia, his idyllic birthplace.

At her transformation, Callisto put up her arms to beg for mercy, but already they were sprouting fur and her fingers were growing claws. Eyes narrowed, lips thickened, ears elongated. Callisto yearned to explain how her virginity had been stolen by Zeus, but all she could emit were low growls. She lumbered deep into the woods, engulfed by misery. She was frightened of her old hunting companions, frightened of other bears, frightened of wolves. Her father Lycaon could be running with the pack, but how could he recognize her? Adding to Callisto's woe was the loss of her baby and the indifference of Zeus.

Arcas was unaware of his origins. He had become a splendid hunter and one day in his fifteenth year encountered his bear parent. Callisto knew him at once. She gazed at him fixedly with her yellow eyes, willing him to recognize her. She reared and approached her son slowly, waving her paws, yearning to embrace him. Callisto strained to reveal her identity, but could only growl. The terrified boy raised his spear to kill her. Zeus took pity on his former love and caught the lethal weapon as it sped toward the bear's heart. Then the All Powerful, through a gap in the winds, whisked them up to the starry skies and set them as the constellations Great Bear and Little Bear.

But Hera, the jealous Queen of Olympus, was displeased to see a rival exalted rather than eternally punished. She persuaded the sea gods to forbid the Bears cool drink or refreshing baths. That is why Ursa Major and Ursa Minor are circumpolar, wheeling around and around the sky but never, like other stars, sinking below the watery horizon.

In honor of Callisto, a cult in ancient Athens celebrated the annual Brauron, the Bear Festival. In the temple of Artemis little girls between the ages of five and ten dressed and acted as bears, growling and running wild. The holiday celebrated the farewell to untamed childhood, the approach of womanhood, and Greek ideas of civilized behavior.

DIVINE
WHITE MARE

A FEW MILES south of Uffington, incised into the chalk bedrock of the hilly English countryside, stretches the gigantic figure of a horse at full gallop. Angular and abstract, elegant and mysterious, the white form measures 374 feet from muzzle to tail. Experts believe it dates from the late Bronze Age, about 1000 BCE, and may be a tribute to Epona, the ancient Celtic horse goddess. Now largely shrouded by time, the "Divine White Mare" had epochs of glory.

Epona worship arose in Gaul, flourished with the conquering Romans and traveled with the legions throughout Britain. The goddess was especially worshipped by the cavalry and turned up everywhere in Roman stables and barracks. Somewhere in the rafters an icon of Epona and her horses would turn up, sometimes depicted with foals on her lap. She often holds a basket of corn or fruit, especially apples. Sometimes Epona is riding, always "lady style," never astride. She may be lying back along the horse but never sidesaddle—the goddess sits the horse on the side as if on a chair, legs dangling over the animal's flanks.

The deity loved roses, and soldiers believed that decked with garlands of the fragrant flower she worked protective magic. Tiny clay images of Epona were available for travel, tucked into tunics or saddle trappings for luck in battle.

Charioteers were the athletes of the military, and they too relied on Epona to keep them safe in the perilous sport. Eight annual Equirra celebrations in holiday-mad Rome honored horses, the chief festivity dedicated to Epona on December 18. The daredevils drove two- or four-horse chariots around a tight oval in the Circus Maximus, cheered on by over two thousand bloodthirsty spectators. It took immense skill not to be hurled out on the turns; an official on the sidelines threw water on the smoking wheels. For the victor, a laurel wreath, palm and glory. For Epona, adoration.

On horseback or off, mother for all

Other than as battle goddess, the White Mare has profound dominions especially appealing to women. Epona also personifies an early fertility goddess, a protective deity, in icons offering the symbolic horn of plenty. Sometimes Epona is depicted as a goddess of rivers and thermal springs, a naked water nymph in such shrines. When an Epona image holds a key, she is honored as a psychopomp—guide to the underworld land of the dead. As a crossroads symbol, the goddess is conceived as an intermediary between the living and the dead or between day and night. And especially in Ireland she has a connection with nightmares. Beyond the horse, she is especially protective of oxen, cattle and donkeys, a lover of dogs and birds.

Some viewers perceive the Uffington figure as a dragon rather than a horse, perhaps the site of the battle with St. George. Who knows? It is difficult to reconstruct the mind set of Iron Age people and the purpose of such quirky vestiges. But we do know the prodigious figure has inspired awe down the ages. Since ancient times, every seven years the local lord hosted a three-day festival at the spot, fun and games, including wrestling and cheese rolling down the hillsides—how Merrie England is that? The basic purpose of the event was to clean up overgrowth and scour the horse to the whiteness of new blizzard. The celebrations lapsed about a hundred years ago, but the English Heritage is responsible for the site and keeps things nicely pristine, thank you.

ANIMALISTIC EGYPTIAN GODS

THE EGYPTIANS believed that the souls of the departed could assume the form of any living thing or plant, so the gods, who in many respects closely resembled them, could and did take upon themselves the forms of birds and beasts; this was the fundamental idea of so-called Egyptian animal worship, which provoked the merriment of the cultured Greek and drew down upon the Egyptians the ridicule and abuse of the early Christian writers. But if the matter be examined closely, its apparent stupidity disappears. The Egyptians paid honor to certain birds, and animals, and reptiles, because they considered that they possessed certain characteristics of the gods to whom they made them sacred.

The educated Egyptian never worshipped an animal as an animal, but only as an incarnation of a god. The Hebrews, Greeks, and Romans never understood the logical conception which underlay the reverence with which the Egyptians regarded certain animals, and as a result they grossly misrepresented their religion.

—E. A. WALLIS BUDGE, *Egyptian Magic*, 1901

THE ELEPHANT'S CHILD

THIS IS the Elephant's Child having his nose pulled by the Crocodile. He is much surprised and astonished and hurt, and he is talking through his nose and saying, "Led got You are hurtig bet" He is pulling very hard, and so is the Crocodile: but the Bi-Coloured-Python-Rock-Snake is hurrying through the water to help the Elephant's Child. All that black stuff is the banks of the great grey-green greasy Limpopo River (but I am not allowed to paint these pictures), and the bottly-tree with the twisty roots and the eight leaves is one of the fever-trees that grow there.

Underneath the truly picture are shadows of African animals walking into an African ark. There are two lions, two ostriches, two oxen, two camels, two sheep, and two other things that look like rats, but I think they are rock-rabbits. They don't mean anything. I put them in because I thought they looked pretty. They would look very fine if I were allowed to paint them.

Then the Bi-Coloured-Python-Rock-Snake scuffled down from the bank and said, "My young friend, if you do not now, immediately and instantly, pull as hard as ever you can, it is my opinion that your acquaintance in the large-pattern leather ulster" (and by this he meant the Crocodile) "will jerk you into yonder limpid stream before you can say 'Jack Robinson.'"

— RUDYARD KIPLING, *Just So Tales*

THE ELEPHANT'S CHILD

EUROPA AND THE BULL

WHILE PICKING flowers with her maidens along the shore, Europa, princess of Sidon, saw a beautiful bull, white as untrodden snow. Timid at first, she presently held out a bunch of flowers and the creature licked her hand. Then she called to her companions: "Come, dear playmates…let us mount the bull here and take our pastime, for truly, he will bear us on his back, and carry all of us; and how mild he is, and dear, and gentle to behold, and no whit like other bulls!" She mounted him, but before her companions could follow, the bull leaped up and sped toward the sea. The beautiful beast was Zeus in disguise, who had fallen in love with Europa and had assumed this form to carry her off. He swam to Crete and there Europa became the mother of Minos, the great Cretan king, and of Rhadamanthus, the judge of the dead in the underworld.

—MOSCHUS, *Idyls, II*, 150 BCE

133
EUROPA AND THE BULL

THE FOX WIFE

O NO WAS the loneliest soul in the village of Mino. Not one girl slipped into his heart, however much he yearned for a wife. In his mind lingered a picture of ideal female beauty, but what he saw around him displeased Ono. This one was too fat, that one was too thin, this one chattered too much, that one was silent as a grave, another was such a bad cook she was a disgrace to rice.

At last one day in the forest he saw the beautiful woman he had dreamed of all his life. He married her and when time passed rejoiced at the birth of a son. Simultaneously Ono's dog gave birth to a puppy. As it grew, the little dog became more and more unfriendly to the lady of the forest, snarling and showing its sharp little teeth. She begged her husband to kill it, but Ono refused to shed the blood.

At last the dog attacked her so viciously that she was frightened and resumed her former shape. She again became a fox,

leaped over the fence and fled. Suddenly Ono realized he had
married a *kitsune*. "You may be a fox," Ono yelled after her,
"but you are the mother of my son and I love you. Come back
whenever you please, I will always welcome you." So every
evening she returns as his wife and sleeps in his arms. But every
morning a fox leaves the cottage, leaps the fence and runs back
into the forest.

—ADAPTED FROM AN ANCIENT JAPANESE FOLK TALE

THE FOX WIFE

NOUNS OF VENERY

AN ANIMAL GROUP DESIGNATION

THE ENGLISH are obsessed with hunting, from royalty on magnificent horses to kids playing in the woods with popguns. The earliest printed books treated the subject. Many volumes included the delightful terms customary to designate animal groups. The lists were called Nouns of Venery (an Old French word for the art of hunting) or Nouns of Assemblage. The *Book of St. Albans*, published in 1486, contained 164 such terms. The following selection offers our favorites from that source.

> Antelopes: a herd
> Apes: a shrewdness
> Asses: a pace
> Badgers: a cete
> Bears: a sloth
> Bees: a swarm

Birds: a flock
Boars: a sounder
Bucks: a brace
Cats: a clowder
Cattle: a drove
Chickens: a brood
Cranes: a sedge
Crows: a murder
Cubs: a litter
Deer: a herd
Elks: a gang
Ferrets: a fesnyng
Fishes: a shoal
Flies: a swarm
Foxes: a skulk
Goats: a trip
Goldfinches: a charm
Hares: a down
Hawks: a cast
Horses: a harras
Hounds: a pack
Kangeroos: a troop
Kittens: a kindle
Larks: an exaltation
Leopards: a leap
Lions: a pride

Mares: a stud
Moles: a labor
Monkeys: a troop
Mules: a barren
Nightingales: a watch
Owls: a parliament
Peacocks: a muster
Ponies: a string
Porpoises: a school
Pups: a litter
Ravens: an unkindness
Seals: a pod
Sheep: a flock
Squirrels: a dray
Starlings: a murmuration
Swallows: a flight
Swans: a bevy

Toads: a knot
Turtles: a bale
Whales: a gam
Wolves: a rout
Woodpeckers: a descent

GIFTED HUMANS

NOTHING delights a lover of animals and the occult more than a tale about the rare human who is blessed with a mysterious ability to communicate with wild creatures. Gavin Maxwell in his book *Ring of Bright Waters* described this quality possessed by his neighbor on the lonely northwest coast of Scotland, a woman "of fine-drawn iron beauty softened by humor" named Morag Murdu.

"What little success I myself have with animals is due, I think, solely to patience, experience, and a conscious effort to put myself in the animal's position, but I do not think that any of these things have been necessary to Morag. She frankly finds more to like and to love in animals than in human beings, and they respond to her immediately as if she were one of themselves, with a trust and respect that few of us receive from our own kind. I am convinced that there exists between her and them some rapport that is not for achievement, even by long perseverance, of the bulk of those humans who would wish it. It would not, perhaps, be difficult to find more understandable explanations for individual cases in which, with her, this rapport seems apparent, but it is the number of these cases, and the consistency with which the animal's behaviour departs from its established pattern towards mankind, that convinces me of something not yet explainable in existing terms."

Leonard Woolf in his autobiography *Growing* recalls "a curious incident which I saw take place in the bungalow by the sea." The time is 1905, the place Ceylon where Woolf shared quarters with another civil servant named Templer. Both men loved animals and soon acquired a menagerie, beginning with five dogs.

"I have often heard of people who have a magnetic power over animals, but this is the only time in my life that I have seen an exhibition of it. Templer had a fox terrier bitch which normally was completely good-tempered and obedient. She had a litter of puppies in a basket in the corner of our bathroom and the moment they were born she went madly savage, refusing to allow anyone, including Templer, to come into the room. The moment that Templer tried to go in she flew at him and in the narrow space he found it impossible to get hold of her without being severely bitten. I tried with the same result. Next day an engineer who was in charge of a large irrigation work in the Northern Province looked in on us. He was a big, dark, gentle, shy, silent man called Harward. We told him what was happening in the bathroom and he asked us what we wanted done with the bitch and her puppies. We said we wanted to get her and her basket into another room so we could use the bathroom. He said that he thought he could manage that. He opened the door of the bathroom. The bitch immediately sat up in the basket growling; Harward walked straight up to her, patted her on the head and made her lie down, and carried the basket with the whole family quietly in it into the other room."

A famous American author was blessed with the unusual gift described by William Sharp, British poet.

"Henry David Thoreau during his two years in Walden woods came to know beasts, birds and fishes with an intimacy more extraordinary than was the case with St. Francis of Assisi. Birds came at his call, and forgot their hereditary fear of man; beasts lipped and caressed him; the very fish in lake

141

and stream would glide, unfearful, between his hands. With children he was affectionate and gentle, with old people and strangers considerate. He loved his kind as animals, but did not seem to find them as interesting as those furred and feathered."

THE INSPIRATIONAL HORSE

EONS AGO, Hawaii arose from the churning waters of the Pacific Ocean, shook itself off and formed dry land under the brilliant gaze of the sun. All in good time animals appeared; chickens, pigs, goats. Each knew that it had a guardian spirit. Their belief never wavered, despite sometimes harsh treatment by masters. When matters with a mistreated animal got crucial, a spirit might appeal to the gods for help. For the beasts themselves, a taboo forbade them to commune with gods. The noble animals lent themselves patiently in service to humankind, assured that at the end of life loving spirits would guide them into the realm of radiant peace.

So stood matters until the foreigners stomped in, adventurers from the mysterious lands of Europe. The arrivals brought with them a new element, the horse. As these animals had never lived there, they had not acquired a guardian spirit nor had their masters the wits to pray for one. The beasts suffered.

They labored with scant returns, working faithfully as horses do, and sometimes were treated harshly. To add to their distress, in the humid jungly climate the sun shone hotter than the horses could tolerate and they missed their homeland. The present time offered no joy and all they could look forward to was more of the miserable same. But when they learned about what the guardian spirits bestowed on other animals, the horses too craved a happy afterlife—ease, lush meadows, cool springs. Best of all, no masters.

Gloom like a black cloak settled over the equine community, but one day the inspiration of a small mare shone forth. Ullikana could not see her peers suffer any longer. Her dearest friend was dying and without a guardian spirit how could the body pass the gates to the place great and good?

A natural-born activist, Ullikana assembled the other horses in her stable for a meeting. "I CANNOT BEAR THIS LIFE ANY LONGER," she raved, stamping a hoof and snorting like a crazy creature. "And when my friend dies, who will guide her into the next world? Who will take care of us when our time comes? Our masters will not plead on our behalf and we must take the risk and do it ourselves. If we offend the gods by breaking the taboo, what do we have to lose? If they kill us, we will be spared some woeful years."

The horses shivered in fear at the thought of the forbidden act, but logic was on the side of Ullikana. They looked at the dying animal lying in the hay, her sides heaving, breathing with effort, whimpering faintly in pain. The sight gave the horses courage, but haste was needed to save her soul. They filed outside led by Ullikana into the warm silent night, dimly lit by a crescent moon. All whispered prayers, trembling so hard they could barely walk and forming a circle. The horses faced outside the ring, tails entwined, so as not to offend the gods by the sight of their backsides.

As the animals gained confidence, their benedictions gained strength and arose to the heavens. Suddenly out of the dark sky a soft blue light began to emerge in the distance. It floated toward them and hovered, flickering over the ring of transfixed bodies. With a great whoosh of feathers unfolding the

THE INSPIRATIONAL HORSE

sphere of light burst into magnificent form—a blue horse with huge silver wings.

"I am your guardian spirit," it told them in loving tones. "The gods granted your wish, as ever they are inclined to do with ardent prayers. My eyes and heart will be connected with your kind for eternity," it vowed. The spirit walked into the stable and gently enfolded the dying mare in its glowing wings. The horses, courteous creatures ever, looked away, as is proper to a sacred moment. The whimpering ceased. When the horses opened their eyes, the ghost of Ullikana's friend, ready for the next world, was following the blue spirit. The wraith said her farewells to Ullikana and added, "Do not cry. We will meet again in the next world along with all our kind, thanks to your wisdom and courage. Throughout all the islands and into a greater world, you will always be remembered as the savior of Hawaiian horses."

THE LOGIC
OF DRAGONS

LET US PASS now from the zoo of reality to the zoo of mythologies, to the zoo whose denizens are not lions but sphinxes and griffins and centaurs.

We are ignorant of the meaning of the dragon in the same way that we are ignorant of the meaning of the universe, but there is something in the dragon's image that fits man's imagination, and this accounts for the dragon's appearance in different places and periods.

—JORGE LUIS BORGES

MAGPIES
GOOD BIRDS, BAD BIRDS

AGPIES often receive a bad press, perhaps because of an ancient belief that seemed to spring out of nowhere. Some people were convinced that magpies, of all God's creatures, were the only ones to forego the comfort of the interior Ark. They opted for perching by themselves atop the vessel, chattering maliciously at the animals huddled within. Add to this a legend that magpies were the only *Corvidae* refusing to don full mourning dress on the day of Christ's crucifixion. Their kin, ravens and crows, attended in sober black; magpies as usual were pied with white.

From such folklore we can see why these birds are met with some ambivalence. It is considered unlucky to kill magpies, and in certain areas of Europe the birds are honored for the chattering that warns of approaching wolves. In Scotland, however, they are regarded as the Devil's own bird, believed to have an unholy drop of his blood under their tongues. In Scotland and England it is unlucky to see one flying away from the sun. Whoever does so should grab the first object that comes to hand, throw it after the bird and say, "Bad luck to the bird that flies widdershins."

Old ways exist believed to avert a malevolent magpie sighting: Raise your hat in salutation. Form a cross with your foot on the ground (or as many crosses as magpies). Wet your forefinger with spittle and make the sign of the cross on your shoe. Spit on the ground three times and say, "Devil, Devil, I defy thee! Magpie, Magpie, I go by thee!"

A single magpie is especially associated with bad luck. Only one bird croaking persistently around a house, for instance, sounds the death knell of an occupant. Two magpies foretell good luck, although it is still necessary to salute the duo by bowing or spitting to ensure that the auspicious omen will be fulfilled.

A childhood rhyme indicates the ambivalent and magical nature of the magpie sightings: One for sorrow / Two for joy / Three for a girl / Four for a boy / Five for silver / Six for gold / Seven for a secret / Never to be told.

—SARAH SIMPSON-ENOCK

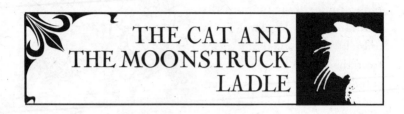

THE CAT AND THE MOONSTRUCK LADLE

ONCE UPON a time there lived a sly old woman adept at preying on others. She delighted in tricky schemes to separate her family and neighbors from their money. When her nephew married a simple country lass, Granny Greedle viewed the bride as a new pigeon. During her first visit, the old woman asked red-cheeked Letty if she was disturbed by the scratching in the walls. "What scratching?" the young woman asked. "I don't hear any scratching."

"Why, you have mice," said the crafty old lady. "They will get into your bread and cheese and foul all your food."

There were no mice, but the old woman had implanted mice into the brain of the bride and soon she thought she heard scratching. The following day the old woman arrived with a black-and-white cat. "This is my own sweet Grimalkin," she said, "he thrives on killing mice, the darling. He will rid your house and in a few days I will come to take him home."

About an hour later the cat had vanished, and Letty assumed that he had found his way home. Grimalkin did return home and the old woman hid him in a neighbor's barn. Several days later she returned to the bride and asked for the cat. "He disappeared the day he came," said the young woman, "and I was sure he had run home."

"I haven't seen hide nor hair of him!" Granny Greedle screamed. "My house is plagued with mice, a dozen at once ran off with half a Cheshire cheese." Tears ran down her wrinkles. "I have reared him from a kitten and there has never been

TH CAT AND THE MOONSTRUCK LADLE

such a nonesuch for killing mice. Once he caught two at once, one with his left paw, one with his right."

The old woman added that a cat spotted like that was a rarity in the village and gave rise to the old saying:

> *A coal-black cat with snowy loins,*
> *Is worth its weight in silver coins.*

Then Granny Greedle stomped out, assuring the lass that by this measure Grimalkin was worth fifteen pounds of silver coins.

Letty was astounded at the value put on the cat. She consulted her father-in-law, who was aware of the old woman's larcenous character. "Did she ever borrow anything from you?" Letty asked.

"Oh, once long ago she borrowed an old wooden ladle not worth one farthing," he told her. "That was all ever." But Letty ran off, satisfied.

A feline felony

When Granny Greedle turned up the next day to collect the silver, the bride asked for the ladle. The old lady expressed surprise and said that children had been playing with the ladle in the dirt and that it had been used for kindling.

"Since you want value for the cat and I want value for the ladle, there is nothing for it but to go before a magistrate," Letty said.

Granny Greedle chuckled to herself at the stupidity of country girls. Since it was clear that a cat was worth more than a wooden ladle, she was certain to win the case and add the silver coins to the stash under her feather bed.

In the courtroom the young woman courteously let the old woman go first. Granny Greedle sang the virtues of Grimalkin, the marvel of catdom. She raved, she ranted, never in the history of the world had there ever been such a peerless feline. The cat, she assured the judge, was worth a thousand ladles and all she was asking for was a mere fifteen pounds of silver.

Rustics sometimes learn shrewdness from the proximity of foxes. Letty claimed that the value of the cat was way offset by the value of the ladle.

In the moon overhead, at its full, you can see
The trunk, branch and leaf of a cinnamon tree.

One windy night a branch from such a tree had been blown down in front of her father-in-law's cottage and he had whittled a ladle from the moonstruck wood. Whatever the ladle was dipped into—soup, beer, money—never decreased. The contents remained the same despite the amount on the ladle, Letty assured the judge. And the old woman had thrown that wondrous ladle into the fire!

The judge, on hearing this absurd tale, understood that the marvels of the cat had been a pretext for extortion. He ruled that the two claims canceled each other out. Granny Greedle glared at Letty and stalked off, outsmarted by a country girl and deprived of gainful unemployment.

—ADAPTED FROM AN ENGLISH FOLK TALE

AN ODD OUTCOME

LBRECHT DÜRER'S woodcut illustrates a medieval legend about the sly Fox who upon occasion joins time to turn the Wheel of Fate. Noble birds, creatures of the ancient gods and highly respected—the Eagle of Zeus, Hera's Peacock, and the Falcon of Horus—unaccountably lose their prestige. Common rascals represented by the Jay, Magpie, and Pheasant (all three noted for their thievery) perch high in public esteem with the Magpie crowned king. The woodcut's comment of society is as valid today as it was during the Middle Ages. Never mind. The cunning Fox has a short attention span and Time will once again turn the Wheel without his devious assistance.

OSCAR
THE FAREWELL CAT

SCAR IS known and loved the length and breadth of Rhode Island, and his story is creeping on little cat feet into larger venues. The amazing creature is two years old, rescued from an animal shelter as a kitten. Oscar resides in a unique environment and has created his own unique function.

The cat's home is the advanced dementia unit of the Steere House Nursing and Rehabilitation Center in Providence, which houses the terminally ill. When Oscar senses that a patient is about to pass away, he swings into a mysterious course of action. The cat pads his way down the corridors and jumps onto the patient's bed where he remains, cuddling and purring, until the moment of death. No longer needed, he leaves quietly and pads back to his own devices. Oscar's instinct is unerring. He has mewed such strange farewells in twenty-five cases, and each time the patient has died within hours. The cat's comforting vigil alerts the medical staff into summoning family members who may want to offer a final goodbye and perhaps arrange for last rites. Geriatrician Dr. David M. Dosa reported about Oscar in *The New England Journal of Medicine*: "His presence," Dosa stated, "has been a comfort to many family members."

The hospice houses five other cats, all of whom go about usual feline lives indifferent to terminal events. What can account for Oscar's singular sensibility? A good clue from WebMD: "I think there are certain chemicals released when someone is dying, and he is smelling and sensing those," says Dr. Joan Teno of Brown University, who also tends patients at the hospice. A reasonable explanation for the initial alert. But Oscar the beloved Farewell Cat offers an eerie, almost humane, understanding of "compassionate end-of-life care," for which he is honored on a plaque outside Steere House.

PLATERO

JUAN RAMON JIMENEZ preferred his donkey above all other animals and most people. With Platero, the poet rode forth daily like an earthy Don Quixote and observed life in his Andalusian village. From simple images, lofty thoughts arise.

At Angelus, a donkey and roses

Look, Platero, how many roses are falling all around; blue roses, white roses, roses without color. One would think that the sky were dissolving into roses. Look how the roses are covering my forehead, my shoulders, my hands. What shall I do with so many roses?

Do you know, I wonder, for I do not, where this delicate flower comes from? Daily it casts a mantle of tenderness over the landscape, leaving it softly pink, white and blue...more roses, more roses…like a painting by Fra Angelico who always knelt to paint the sky.

One would think that they were throwing roses to the earth from the seven galleries of Paradise. Like a warm and lightly colored snowfall the roses lie on the tower, on the roof, on the trees. Look: all strong lines, with their adornment, become delicate. More roses, more and more roses.

It seems, Platero, while the Angelus is ringing, that this life of ours loses its daily force and that another force from within, loftier, purer and more constant, causes everything to rise, like fountains of grace, to the stars which are beginning to sparkle now among the roses. More roses. Your eyes, which you cannot see, Platero, and which you raise meekly to the sky, are two beautiful roses.

—JUAN RAMON JIMENEZ, *Platero and I: An Andalusian Elegy*

159

THE PUPPY WAR

RIBAL CONFLICT over a puppy had huge consequences, according to the Tuscarora Indians. In the beginning of time, all mortals spoke the same language. The biggest village, ruled by the heroine Godasiyo, was divided by a river with a sturdy bridge. One fine day Godasiyo's dog gave birth to seven puppies, the last of the litter outstanding. The little dog was gleaming white with black markings, clever, playful, magical. He was the most adorable puppy the world had ever seen and people loved to see and pet the remarkable creature.

The tribe on the other side of the river burned with jealousy. A violent clash broke out. Godasiyo intended to calm matters by burning the bridge, but still the rivals menaced. She decided to move her people and the puppy to a unified place where everyone could enjoy the little dog in peace. Godasiyo invented the canoes to transport them. But when the Canoes came to a further division in the river, contention broke out again. This way? That way?

Fights broke out and in the fray Godasiyo and the puppy fell into the water and drowned. They were reborn instantly, the heroine as a big sturgeon and the puppy as a little whitefish. When the people wanted to chatter about the miracle, they could no longer understand each other. The many languages that divide humanity exist because of strife over a puppy.

RAINBOW SNAKE AND THE LAUGHING FROGS

AUSTRALIAN ABORIGINES tell us of the power of Rainbow Snake and the frogs that helped to create the animate world. Until their advent, the planet was featureless. Nothing was manifest, but even a zero is fraught with possibilities. During the creative Dreamtime, earlier than we can imagine, ancestral spirits activated.

Gigantic Rainbow Snake pushed her way out of the earth to the surface, shoving aside everything in her path. The serpent slithered through the continent creating valleys and mountains. When she got tired, Rainbow Snake coiled up and slept, forming water holes deep in the earth. After the snake had left tracks everywhere, she hissed for the frogs. A multitude of the creatures hopped out and assembled, their chubby stomachs full of water. Rainbow Snake tickled the frogs and they laughed. Water gushed from their mouths, filling the snake's tracks, forming rivers and lakes. Then grass and trees raised their green fingers and the earth began to tremble with life.

The Rainbow Snake vanished, generally visible only as a murky streak in the Milky Way. But the genetic serpent sometimes reveals herself as a rainbow moving through water and rain, enameled skin luminous. Still she shapes landscapes and waterways, naming places, singing of places. Be advised. It is well to beware the serpent's playtime, for she may drown and swallow mortals. But feeling benevolent, Rainbow Snake confers on certain wise ones powers of healing and rainmaking.

— BARBARA STACY, ADAPTED FROM
AN AUSTRALIAN ABORIGINE MYTH

ANIMALS SACRED TO ROMAN DEITIES

Apollo: the wolf, the griffin, and the crow

Bacchus: the dragon and the panther

Diana: the stag and the cat

Hercules: the deer

Juno: the peacock and the lamb

Jupiter: the eagle

Mars: the horse and the vulture

Mercury: the cock

Minerva: the owl

Neptune: the bull

Venus: the dove, the swan, and the sparrow

Vulcan: the lion

SERENE
SEABIRDS,
CALM SEAS

HE ROMAN poet Ovid recounts this magical old Greek tale of eternal love embodied in seabirds. Ceyx, King of Thessaly, was the son of Lucifer the Morning Star and as luminously beautiful as his father. Queen Halcyone also sprang from exalted parentage, sired by Aeolus, god of the winds. Now, Ceyx was tormented by the strange death of his brother and determined to consult the oracle of Apollo in Ionia. When the king's intention to set sail became known to his devoted wife, she shuddered and tears coursed down her cheeks.

"Dear husband," said the queen, "the sea terrifies me, the woeful sea, for at my father's castle I have seen the ferocious power of escaped winds that turn waves into mountains. And lately I have seen wrecks of planks on the beach, an ill omen. But if you will not heed my fears and stay, at least let me sail with you. Then we may travel and return or be storm tossed together, for without you I cannot live."

Ceyx returned Halcyone's blazing love and dreaded the separation also, but he would neither forego the oracle nor expose his beloved to peril. He embraced his wife and kissed her tenderly, trying to allay her fears. But Halcyone was solaced only when he promised to return, should the fates allow it, before the moon circled twice.

She clung to Ceyx as they walked slowly down to the dock, and bade him a sad farewell in a trembling voice. His crew manned the oars, and Halcyone gazed seaward as the vessel receded and only the sails remained visible. When all had vanished from the horizon, she returned to the castle and threw herself down to weep on the couch still redolent of their love.

Ceyx had reached half his course when Jupiter, in need of diversion, raised his fist and loosed the triple thunderbolt. The sky blackened, the sea whitened. A frenzied hurricane with waves as high as castles tossed the boat up to the skies, then flung it down like a spoiled child tired of a toy. As the waters engulfed his head, Ceyx's last thought was of Halcyone. That night she had a hideous nightmare and knew that her beloved had met a watery death. Halcyone wailed so loudly that she woke herself.

At dawn Halcyone fled to the shore, to the dock where the couple had said their farewells, kissing as they strolled. As she looked seaward to where she had last seen his boat, a dot appeared on the horizon. Unlike the boat sailing away she had watched getting smaller and smaller, this dim object grew bigger as she gazed. Then Halcyone could make out a body floating in on the waves, and as it neared she trembled to recognize Ceyx. "Dear husband," she cried in wonder, "how come you to return to me like this?"

Determined to join Ceyx in his watery death, Halcyone leaped from the high sea wall. "Then she found herself flying, beating the air with wings newly formed," Ovid assures us. Covered with feathers she flew, twittering sorrowful sounds as of lamentations. When the bird reached the corpse, she engulfed the white limbs in feathery softness and frantically kissed the cold mouth over and over with her beak. Now the goddess Juno took pity on Halcyone, who knows why, and suddenly the lifeless form fluttered, sprouted feathers and Ceyx too became a bird.

They are still to be seen, always together, flying or riding the waves, as loving as ever they were. Each winter they build a nest afloat on the water, and for seven days Halcyone spreads her wings over their eggs. Then Aeolus keeps the winds in check to protect his grandchildren, the sea is tamed, and sailors rejoice at the halcyon days.

—ADAPTED FROM *Greek Gods in Love* BY BARBARA STACY

WHY CROWS
ARE BLACK

POLLO fell in love with Coronis, a princess of Thessaly. He was determined to have his way with her, but despite the god's beauty Coronis refused him. She was in love with Ischys, an Arcadian prince. And unlikely as it seems that she preferred her mortal lover to the glorious god, love is a mysterious force. Eros shoots where he shoots, golden arrows fly, causing much consternation in the world. A story everlasting. When Coronis was with child, Apollo set off on a journey to Delphi but set a crow to spy on her. At that time all crows were white. These birds make terrific spies, for they have sharp eyes and jeering voices.

When Apollo reached Delphi, an oracle told him that at that very moment Coronis was enjoying her princely lover. Just then the crow flew in, chattering as fast as his beak could move, insane with excitement, reporting the scandal. "It is all your fault, you brainless bird," Apollo raged, "for not watching her closely enough." The god cursed the bird with such fury that its feathers were scorched. And all crows have been black ever after.

—ADAPTED FROM *Greek Gods in Love* BY BARBARA STACY

WHY CROWS ARE BLACK

WOLF OF DRASTIC PROPHECY

ENRIR was a hugely monstrous wolf, in ancient mythology predicted to inflict destruction on the world and on the Aesir, the Norse gods. He was the son of the deity Loki and the giantess Angrboda. When Fenrir was a pup, the gods became aware of the doomsday prophecy and determined to forestall it. But even as a youngster Fenrir was such a terrifying force that the gods themselves feared his powers. Slaying him seemed the obvious answer, for gods rather enjoyed a little festive spattering of blood. But Loki was a trickster and formidable. It was a foregone conclusion that he would wreak havoc if his son was killed.

Finally the Aesir decided to simply confine Fenrir forever. They managed to fetter the half-grown wolf and lock him in a cage. Only Tyr, the fearless God of War, would go near enough to feed and care for Fenrir. The gods noticed that the wolf was growing at an alarming rate and soon would be able to burst forth to freedom. The deities knew they had to do something soon to render him harmless before he reached monstrous size. They formed a crafty plan and prepared three chains. The first, very strong, was called Leyding. The Aesir brought it to Fenrir and suggested that he try his strength with it. The wolf, proud of his brawn and believing he could snap it, permitted them to shackle him. At Fenrir's first powerful kick the chain broke and Fenrir released himself from Leyding.

The gods made a second fetter, twice as strong, and named it Dromi. They asked Fenrir to try the new engineering marvel and if he could break it, his fame for strength would resound down the ages. The wolf knew that his might had increased since Leyding and agreed to take the risk. Shackled again, Fenrir shook himself, strained himself, and kicking hard snapped the chain, breaking it into pieces that flew through the air. To this day in Scandinavia people say "loose from Leyding" or "strike out of Dromi" when they mean to express achieving something with great effort.

Now the gods began to fear that the wolf might be impossible to contain, for even gods may fear a monster of such dire prophecy. Now red-bearded Odin weighed in like heavy artillery. He realized that only a magic chain could keep the monster bound. The God of Thunder sent for underground dwarves, artisans of the gods, and explained the problem. The dwarves trudged

WOLF OF DRASTIC PROPHECY

away and returned weeks later with Gleipner, a lovely ribbon, thin, soft and shining. Despite its deceptive appearance the ribbon was incredibly strong, fashioned of six strange elements — the footstep of a cat, the roots of a mountain, a woman's beard, the breath of fishes, the sinews of a bear, a bird's spittle.

When Fenrir saw the ribbon, he suspected a trick. And yet — and yet — it seemed so fragile, so easy for the strength of a monster to tear. Had he not bested the gods with the heavy iron chains of Leyding and Dromi? The odd new test was irresistible for the vain beast, but he was still wary of treachery.

"As a gesture of mutual trust," Fenrir declared with a toothy wolfish smile, "I would like a pledge of good faith. One of you will put a hand into my jaws while I encounter this new trial." None of the gods expressed enthusiasm for the invitation. Finally Tyr, bravest of the divinities, arose and thrust his right hand into Fenrir's mouth. The gods bound Fenrir with the ribbon. No matter how hard he struggled, the wolf could not free himself from Gleipner. The more he strained, the tighter the band grew. At this everyone laughed except Tyr. With a growl that shook the rocks, in revenge the monster bit off the hand that had fed him all his life. The wrist, where Fenrir had bitten, has become known as the "wolf joint."

The gods carried off Fenrir and chained him to a rock a mile down into the earth. To prevent his biting they placed "a certain sword" in his mouth, the hilt on the lower jaw and the point on the upper jaw. Fenrir "howled horribly," saliva ran from his mouth and formed the Van, the River of Hope. There Fenrir will lie flowing the torrent until he becomes unbound on the Gotterdammerung, the Day of Doom for the cosmos.

MAGIC STORIED CREATURES

In the beginning of all things, wisdom and knowledge were with the animals; for Tirawa, the One
Above, did not speak directly to man. He sent
certain animals to tell man that he showed himself
through the beasts, and that from them, and from
the stars and the sun and the moon, man should
learn. Tirawa spoke to man through his works.

— CHIEF LETAKOTS-LESA

Other books available from
www.TheWitchesAlmanac.com

The Horned Shepherd

Wander the magical world of the Valley of Fine Fleeces with a fascinating cast of characters. Meet Big Anna, keeper of both the pagan flame and Cross; a Princess aflame for a strange lover; an Egyptian Priest, steward of mysteries; Friar Paul, lean and sinister; and Saccabe the Black Goat, Father of Many Flocks. Above all you will encounter the mysterious Shepherd of supernatural radiance, among whose curls nestle two small soft horns. Events converge in the forest on Midsummer Eve at full moon as celebrants arrive with meat, bread and wine for the Feast. The Wise Ones recognize the Horned Shepherd as an ancient fertility god who should be sacrificed to enrich the land. Beautiful woodcuts enhance the 146-page book.

Greek Gods in Love

New versions of timeless love tales—lively, witty, entertaining. The author casts a marvelously original eye on the beloved stories of Greek deities, replete with amorous oddities and escapades. Lavishly illustrated with 190 designs drawn from ancient Greek art. Visual delights abound.

Witches All

Perfect for study or casual reading, *Witches All* is a collection from The Witches' Almanac publications of the past. Arranged by topics, the book, like the popular almanacs, is thought provoking and often spurs me on to a tangent leading to even greater discovery.

ABC of Magic Charms

A treasury of amulets, talismans, fetishes and other lucky objects compiled by the staff of *The Witches' Almanac.* An invaluable guide for all who respond to the call of mystery and enchantment.

Love Charms

Love has many forms, many aspects. Ceremonies performed in witchcraft celebrate the joy and the blessings of love. Here is a collection of love charms to use now and ever after.

Ancient Roman Holidays

The glory that was Rome awaits you in Barbara Stacy's classic presentation of a festive year in pagan times. Here are the gods and goddesses as the Romans conceived them, accompanied by the annual rites performed in their worship. Scholarly, light-hearted — a rare combination.

Celtic Tree Magic

Robert Graves in *The White Goddess* writes of the significance of trees in the old Celtic lore. *Celtic Tree Magic* is an investigation of the sacred trees in the remarkable Beth-Luis-Nion alphabet; their role in folklore, poetry, and mysticism.

Moon Lore

As both the largest and the brightest object in the night sky, and the only one to appear in phases, the Moon has been a rich source of myth for as long as there have been mythmakers.

Magic Spells and Incantations

Words have magic power. Their sound, spoken or sung, has ever been a part of mystic ritual. From ancient Egypt to the present, those who practice the art of enchantment have drawn inspiration from a treasury of thoughts and themes passed down through the ages.

Love Feasts

Creating meals to share with the one you love can be a sacred ceremony in itself. With the witch in mind, culinary adept Christine Fox offers magical menus and recipes for every month in the year.

Random Recollections I, II, III, IV

Pages culled from the original (no longer available) issues of *The Witches' Almanac*, published annually throughout the 1970's, are now available in a series of tasteful booklets. A treasure for those who missed us the first time around; keepsakes for those who remember.

Back issues of The Witches' Almanac *also available.*